"The vulnerability and beauty found in th[...]
breathless as Alia wisely leads the weary [...]
goodness and grace, even in the midst of our [...]
break, and loss. Her exquisite words are a tender touch that resurrect
us in our brokenness to the knowledge that we are deeply seen—and
that even in our weakness there can be life-giving glory and reviving
grace. These are healing pages for hurting hearts and ones I will
return to again and again."

Ann Voskamp, *New York Times* bestselling author of
The Broken Way and *One Thousand Gifts*

"With a voice all her own, Alia Joy writes straight from the heart,
holding nothing back. Her story is honest, raw, brave. Her prose is
beautiful and utterly original. Her insights are deep, forged from
years of living in places and spaces most of us try to avoid. You will
quickly think of ten friends who need to read this book. Then you
will realize the one who needs it most is you. *Glorious Weakness* eases
past our practiced smiles and Christian platitudes to show us what
Paul meant when he wrote, 'For when I am weak, then I am strong'
(2 Cor. 12:10 NIV). By embracing the kind of strength that can be
found only in admitting our weakness, Alia Joy has given us what we
long for above all—hope."

Liz Curtis Higgs, bestselling author of *Bad Girls of the Bible*

"Alia does nothing without soulful intention, and this includes her
writing. Her perspective of the world helps me think broader, hum-
bler, and outside the norm, and I'm grateful for it. She can weave
words as only a skilled artist who has walked long paths to find the
finest thread can. Alia's words are a gift, and we are all better for her
sharing them with us."

Tsh Oxenreider, author of *At Home in the World*

"Alia uses her words to change people. She changes how we see and
more importantly how we act. She gives us the gift of new eyes to
see Jesus in ways and places we didn't expect—and to follow him.
Some people are beautiful writers. Some are powerful motivators.
Alia is both. Her writing is a one-two punch, and we need more of
it in the world."

Lisa-Jo Baker, bestselling author of *Never Unfriended*
and *Surprised by Motherhood*

"*Glorious Weakness* is a beautiful paradox—challenging and comforting, heart-wrenching and heart-mending, devastating and hopeful.

We are all broken. We are all beloved. We all forget both of these are true. Alia's honest, gorgeous words will remind us. I will be thinking about this book for a very long time."

Holley Gerth, bestselling author of *Fiercehearted*

"If your heart is broken, circle around. Alia Joy sets the table and saves a place for the sidelined, the marginalized, and the poor in spirit. Her vulnerable strength paints a compelling picture of Jesus—friend to stragglers, comfort for strugglers. Here's my best advice: lean forward and read this beautiful book with your palms up and your heart open."

Emily P. Freeman, author of *Simply Tuesday* and *The Next Right Thing*

"This book achieves something incredibly powerful and rare: it heals as it cuts. Alia Joy wields her pen like a double-edged sword. For some, her words will inspire the most wonderful Holy Spirit conviction. For others, her message will be a balm of understanding and hope. For all of us, Alia preaches a better, fuller, truer gospel."

Sharon Hodde Miller, author of *Free of Me*

"In her stunning debut, Alia Joy peels the shame from weakness and lights a campfire with the husks, inviting us to gather around and warm our hands. Her vivid, lyrical writing paints a place of solace where longing makes way for belonging and sorrow is a hidden passageway to wonder. I devoured every word. Read this book if you want to believe God is even bigger than you need him to be. There's room for all of us in this wide circle of hope."

Shannan Martin, author of *The Ministry of Ordinary Places* and *Falling Free*

"*Glorious Weakness* is stunningly written, wholly honest, and deeply theological. This book gives words to the feeling we've all had of believing we're on the outside, only to find Jesus with us, beckoning us with a glint in his eyes. Alia Joy's story will help you toss a clichéd Christianity, exchanging it for a vibrant, robust, feet-to-the-ground faith. This is a gift to the body of Christ."

Mary DeMuth, author of *The Seven Deadly Friendships*

"Christians worship One who came as a baby and lived a humble, rejected, and homeless existence. God came as a weak man. How we got to the place where we began to believe—and market—that his kingdom mostly comes through strength is beyond me. This book is a massive leap in the right direction and is long overdue. It is through *weakness*, not our perceived victories and strengths and accomplishments, that the kingdom of Jesus mostly comes in our world. And the sooner we listen to voices like Alia's in her beautiful *Glorious Weakness*, the faster we can get out of the way and God's will can be done here on earth."

A. J. Swoboda, pastor, teacher, and author of *Subversive Sabbath*

"Alia writes with an aching eloquence, inviting us to excavate the places where we are wounded and to sit with our pain and the pain of others. In *Glorious Weakness* she reminds us that God knows where we ache, sees and understands our pain, and wants to heal the many places where we are wounded."

Amena Brown, spoken word poet, host of *HER with Amena Brown* podcast, and author of *How to Fix a Broken Record*

"So often, when I realize sadness or scarcity or silence from God is my lot for a particular season, I find my ego looking for the exit ramp. I have to resist the urge to plead with that silent God for a way out or around. Anything other than through. But God is all about *through*. This book is a beautiful account of the gift of *through*. I am left speechless with wonder and deeply grateful for the incredibly rich gift of weakness in a world that would trick me into believing weakness is anything but glorious."

Deidra Riggs, author, speaker, and disco lover

"Alia Joy's literate prose and fascinating life story as a struggling missionary kid could hardly be more compelling. But it was her visceral honesty and wisdom, particularly about mental health, that pierced me wide awake. She asks, 'What if we started to see weakness not only as something to endure but as our spiritual gift?' If we, the church, can catch this true vision, imagine what we could do!"

Leslie Leyland Fields, author of *The Wonder Years*

"Words are powerful, and Alia Joy wields that power with hard-won, unflinching honesty, patience, and love. She does not sugarcoat the injustices she and her family experienced but invites readers to sit with her in the margins, where so many of us claim to be but so few of us actually are."

Kathy Khang, author of *Raise Your Voice*

"Breathtaking, moving, meaningful, and timely. Alia Joy writes with exquisite skill on topics such as mental illness, suffering, poverty, and weakness—subjects we tend to turn from—and invites her readers in close to experience both the pain and the joy through her honesty, warmth, and hard-won hope in God. She strings words with excellence and beauty, balancing bold courage and humble strength. I highly, highly recommend this book."

Vivian Mabuni, speaker and author of *Warrior in Pink*

"Alia's writing is beautiful, but her content is even more so because it is dripping with counterintuitive truth. In this book, you'll discover that God dwells in the places you least expect. You'll learn of God's glory in the spaces you seldom consider: your weaknesses and deprivations. Alia is a trusted guide, for she knows of what she speaks. I trust the wisdom she has gained from suffering and Jesus Christ in her. This is a timely book, for it directs us to the timeless way of Jesus. May we all heed what she has to say."

Marlena Graves, author of *A Beautiful Disaster*

"With gorgeous prose, Alia Joy takes readers on a guided tour of the intricate twists and turns the human heart can make as it attempts to endure and make sense of suffering. But it's not an abstract treatise about suffering from a ten-thousand-foot view; it's an intimate, vulnerable portrait of her own fragility in the face of poverty, illness, loss, disillusionment, injustice, unrelenting psychic pain, and the take-you-out nature of some forms of hardship. The way she tells her story enables us to become more acquainted with our own. And although this book is about finding God in our weakness, it's also a powerful portrayal of how to ask big, bold, and scary questions about God. She leaves no stone unturned, no room for platitudes or simplistic theologies. Because she does so, readers are empowered to do the same."

Judy Wu Dominick, essayist and speaker

"Alia Joy begins her book by saying it may not be for everyone. Fair enough, and so I began to read. As I turned the final pages I had to disagree with her—no, your book is for all of us, and your timing couldn't be better. In a day when we're witnessing the destructive darkness of power, Alia points to the redeeming light of weakness. Far from a message of 'Woe is me,' she whispers, 'Greater is he.' It is to our benefit to listen."

John Blase, poet and author of *The Jubilee: Poems*

glorious
weakness

glorious weakness

DISCOVERING GOD IN ALL WE LACK

ALIA JOY

BakerBooks

a division of Baker Publishing Group

www.BakerBooks.com

Published by Baker Books
a division of Baker Publishing Group
PO Box 6287, Grand Rapids, MI 49516-6287
www.bakerbooks.com

Printed in the United States of America

Library of Congress Cataloging-in-Publication Data
Names: Joy, Alia, 1978– author.
Title: Glorious weakness : discovering God in all we lack / Alia Joy.
Description: Grand Rapids : Baker Publishing Group, 2019. | Includes
    bibliographical references.
Identifiers: LCCN 2018043233 | ISBN 9780801093340 (pbk.)
Subjects: LCSH: Failure (Psychology)—Religious aspects—Christianity.
Classification: LCC BT730.5 .J69 2019 | DDC 248.8/6—dc23
LC record available at https://lccn.loc.gov/2018043233

19 20 21 22 23 24 25   7 6 5 4 3 2 1

For my dad,
who taught me we can't escape our storytelling
souls, and that sure matters.

For my mom,
who taught me to cherish books and the way
true words move us all closer together.

For Josh,
who's home to me.

For my Jesus,
you come for me again and again,
your goodness astounds me.

Contents

Contents

Foreword

In the summer of 2012, I knelt over the frail shell of a child, my son, strapped to all manner of medical monitoring equipment. His body failing, his frame thinning, the medical staff at Arkansas Children's Hospital was at a loss. They had no answers, no direction. He was an anomaly, they said, and they'd need to regroup after making him as comfortable as possible.

Though the medical community struggled to sort it all out, my faith community seemed to have every answer. God would provide, one said, because God would respond to my great faith. God was setting up a miracle, another said. God works all things together for good, I was reminded. Platitude, platitude, platitude. I smiled through all of them, even nodded. Silently I wondered *Did all those words amount to anything, well-meaning though they were?*

Hunched over my son, all those platitudes haunting, my phone rang. I looked at the screen, read the name. It was a pastor from a more reformed church in my hometown, and as I answered the phone, I wondered what platitude I might hear. There was a purpose in my son's suffering? Everything has a Kingdom purpose? After an exchange of greetings, I clenched my jaw. Stiffened. Braced myself. Through the phone, I heard only three words: "I'm so sorry." There was a pause, and he told me to holler if I needed anything. He said he'd be praying, and that was that.

It was a moment of selfless solidarity, a moment in which this man of the cloth didn't force-feed me anemic answers or sell me some fix-all version of a bright-and-shiny gospel. Instead, he did the work of Christ himself; he entered into my suffering. And years later, after a long season of healing (both my son's and my own), his words served as a reminder of the Christian response to suffering—we enter into it together, share in it together, lament with each other. I suppose it's natural, our tendency to try to run from suffering, to somehow try to drag other folks from their own. We Christians use the holy tools at our disposal (particularly, the misinterpretation of Scripture) in an attempt to pave a path *around* suffering. The problem is that's not the way of Christ. Christ—God with us—entered into the suffering of humanity. He lamented with those who lamented, extended compassion and healing to the hurting. Ultimately, he took on the existential suffering of all mankind as he endured his own suffering on the cross.

The deep invitation of the Christian life is not to a pain-free existence. Instead, the invitation is to enter suffering *with* Christ. But don't take my word for it. (After all, I'm no guru.) Consider these words penned by Oswald Chambers in *My Utmost for His Highest*:

> In the history of the Christian church, the tendency has been to evade being identified with the sufferings of Jesus Christ;

[people] have sought to procure the carrying out of God's order by a shortcut of their own. God's way is always the way of suffering, the way of the "long, long trail."[1]

In these pages, Alia invites us to join her in the "long, long trail" home. Through sexual trauma, encounters with racism, the loss of a child, and mental health issues, Alia shares her suffering with such sensorial artistry that you cannot help but enter in. But this is not a book about suffering for the sake of suffering. Instead, this work leads you deeper into an experience of Christ, the suffering servant, and along the way exposes the faux-christ of middle-class privilege.

Enter this journey soberly, intending to feel it all. As you do, examine your own journey of pain, maybe the pain you've pushed down for so many years. With Alia, experience the Christ who is and always will be *Emmanuel*, God with us, the God who bends low in our suffering and whispers, "I'm so sorry."

Seth Haines, author of *Coming Clean: A Story of Faith*

Introduction

Blessed Are the Poor in Spirit

Every weakness contains within itself a strength.

Sʜūsᴀᴋᴜ Eɴᴅō

This book isn't for everyone. My publisher's marketing team might not want me to tell you that, book sales being what they are these days, especially for a relatively obscure first-time author who is known primarily for writing her feelings on the internet. But there you have it.

When I first had an inkling that I had this book beginning in me, I was bawling my eyes out in the emergency room. (You'll read the details later if you decide this book is, in fact, for you.) I was vulnerable and hurting, thinking of how much of my life I've spent in hospitals. I wrote on my now sorely neglected blog, "I don't want to live like a vagrant anymore, I don't want to be known for my lack, my weakness, my constant recurring despair." I wrote it in the midst of a deep depression when I could barely get out of bed, and my daughter, Kaia, had climbed up next to me, clutched both sides of my face in her tiny palms and said, "I'm sorry you're hurting, Mommy," staring into my tear-filled eyes. I wanted so desperately to tell her I was fine, to pretend again, but I lacked the stamina to even try. It didn't matter to depression that I had a loving and faithful husband in Josh. That Judah, Kaia, and Nehemiah continued growing into kind, compassionate children despite my inability to fix myself. I wanted the meds to work and to not be the kind of person consoled by their children. So this is not the book I'd have chosen for myself—I don't want to be the author who writes about how weak she is.

Truth is, no one wants to be that person. The one always in crisis, the one who is always sick or struggling, the one who always feels like a burden. No one wants to need. No one wants to be found lacking. No one wants a ministry of weakness. In any case, this is the book that started burning a hole in my gut with a message God wouldn't let me shake—that we are all called to a ministry of weakness. That, in fact, we cannot know grace without it.

After that hospital visit, I began meditating on the Scripture found in Matthew 5:3 where Jesus says, "Blessed are the poor in spirit, for theirs is the kingdom of heaven" (NIV). We live in a society that despises lack. We don't value poverty, that's for sure. So what does it mean to be poor in spirit? How could that possibly be what God desires for us? How is it a blessing to *need*?

I've come close to death many times, first with childhood leukemia, but then many more times with chronic and mental illnesses. I've been sick for much of my life. I have bipolar disorder, which, in itself, is often fatal. Something like one in four will lose that battle to suicide. Unfortunately, we don't talk much about suicide in church. When I first wrote the words "bipolar disorder" on my blog, I was terrified. What would people think? But I knew I had family support and generous readers, and so I began writing about faith and mental illness. About sitting with God in the dark. And the emails started coming in.

I discovered that the lights have gone out for many of us. You know how, when you close your eyes, for a moment you can still see the outline of what you were looking at as faint orbs? That's how it felt when the light went out for me: I knew the light had mass and form and it was still there, but I couldn't make out anything. It's the smallest hope of light. And it's that hope of light that I want to share. When the whole world goes dark, even the tiniest glimmer shines.

Looking back at my childhood, I can see that the dark edges always closed in even among the beautiful things, even among the treasures. But now I also see that God continually promises beauty from ashes, redemption from our sorrow.

When I was a girl in the bright and beautiful world, the neighborhood kids and I played pirates. We cut up grocery bags and took the rough brown paper to draw out and place our treasure. We could navigate the world to the correct spot if we just knew where the X was.

To age the maps, my mother, who always indulged our imaginations, taught us how to soak the paper in bitter black tea, to crinkle them up and dry them on the line like a set of fresh linens. The final step was to get an adult and a candle and burn the edges. I was a girl who already knew where the darkest edges in the world were; they curled up and surrounded me, like a map set on fire. They were crisp and black and left your fingers smudged and shadowy like coal. Their char shed like flaking skin and got everywhere. I believed the dark places made me dirty.

But I knew where to dig up the old Folgers coffee can we filled with Mardi Gras beads, plastic gold coins, and baubles we collected. We'd beg our mothers to stop their grocery carts before the parking lot to feed the greedy machines our quarters and turn the metal dial, watching our treasure fall into the slot.

Sometimes we got a fancy emerald ring or a press-on tattoo or a gummy hand that would collect fuzz in our pockets. But we saved each treasure so we'd be able to hide it and find it again.

Once, we sat in the grass on the edge of our lawn with the coffee can peeled open, the whiff of morning percolating while we divided up the good stuff. I slipped a ruby ring onto my finger, looking down at my hand. My flesh was marked with ash from finding my way.

These days, when I am adrift on rough seas of life, and the tidal wave of my own limitations crashes against me, I need the X written down and mapped out so that I can believe in treasure again, to believe in beauty. I need to believe that lost things can be found if we only know where to look. My saltwater tears have mixed with the ash from the Refiner's fire, and they form the ink to pen my story, a story that helps me find my way to the beauty that was always buried and waiting.

I've spent a good bit of my life searching, trying to find my way. Maybe you have too? Maybe you're also marked by the dark edges of your life. Maybe you're tired from going in circles and getting nowhere. Maybe you've lost your way once again and you're not sure you'll ever right this ship. If that's you, this book is the story I offer. My place to simply say, I will not pretend. I will not mask my weakness, my poverty of spirit, my broken places. I will scratch out a story of hope and glory. An X on the map, a cross to guide our way.

So many people don't have a way to talk about these kinds of struggles. The thing is, we all want to be able to tell the truth about ourselves and God. Some of us just didn't know we were allowed.

I hope this book gives you permission to illuminate the darkness in your own life, to skip the shortcut, to weather the storm, and to seek out the treasures along the way. A lot of things don't get said in the Christian Living section of our Bible bookstores or on Christian blogs or in our Bible study groups. Over the years I've written about things like sexual abuse, body image, mental and chronic illness, suicide, doubt, grief, race, poverty, and identity. There's power in truth telling, in resurrecting the sunken things and sifting them, a couple good shakes to get the sand out and let the light back in.

That's what I've attempted to do in this book. I've dug through the stories of my life, and I offer them to you as permission to tell your own, to be honest about the unlikely places God might meet us and to be okay with areas that aren't Sunday-school shiny or put together. This book might read like a memoir because I'm on this journey with you. I haven't "arrived" either, so think of me more as a companion than a guide. It's broken into four parts: weakness, hope, strength, and glory. It is my story of discovering God in all the places I thought were lacking and seeing how he is good when life is anything but. It's about the cycles we live in and the stuff that happens not only before you believe, but long after, when you realize that believing, hoping, and knowing God isn't reciting a sinner's prayer and calling it good. It's remaining fluent in our language of hope on an expedition that often feels foreign and hostile.

It's my hope you'll discover there are miracles and wonder and grace here, but they're often of the small variety. This isn't a book about befores and afters in the extreme-makeover sense, because we live most of our lives in the middle spaces. In the here but not yet of Kingdom Come. But this is a book about life to death and back again. About finding your way, not always out of the darkness, but through it. About surviving the storms and lashing yourself to the bough that will not break—the cross of Christ.

Sometimes trials capsize me, but even in the barrage of waves, tossed to and fro, I know now I have never been unanchored. I am shackled to the grace that lets me breathe under the weight of the tempest. As Charles Spurgeon said: "I have learned to kiss the wave that throws me against the Rock of Ages."[1]

I started out by saying this book wasn't for everyone, and maybe that's true, but its message is. So how do you know if you should keep reading? Well, this book is for every one of you who emailed me and told me my story made you braver with your own, whatever it might be. It's for everyone who doesn't understand their identity as *beloved*. It's for everyone who can't imagine their weakness might be their greatest strength. It's for everyone who thinks strength comes from trying harder and doing more. It's for everyone who struggles and for everyone who loves the struggling. It's for everyone who's sat in the dark with a silent God, looking for a glimmer of hope that they're not alone. It's for everyone who needs to know that being poor in spirit is the richest place of all. That's where the treasure is buried.

Part 1

weakness

one

The Nakedness of Need

The Glorious Weakness of Poverty

We are so inclined to cover up our poverty and
ignore it that we often miss the opportunity
to discover God, who dwells in it.

HENRI J. M. NOUWEN

I have seventeen teeth. Most adults have thirty-two. I count
each one, running my tongue in and out through the hollows
in my jaw, like fence posts that have been pulled, leaving a
rickety mouth full of shame.

The X-ray hangs on the light box to my left, outlining the
ghostly remains. The top left molar has a cavern of black,
and it's this inky blemish that brings me to this chair, tipped
back and bibbed like a helpless infant, tears leaking from
my eyes. It's been weeks to get in and every breath sends
an electric shock down the root of my tooth. My jaw aches

from rolling soft foods to the opposite side of my mouth for so long.

"And you said you had no trauma to the tooth? Nothing hit it or you bit down really hard on something or got hit?"

"No, nothing," I whisper.

"Well, sometimes a tooth can spontaneously die. It does happen. Usually it's from trauma, but sometimes with an infection, it can get into the nerve and down to the root. The nerve is dead and now the infection has gone into your jaw and that's what they saw in the ER a few weeks ago with the CT scan."

I hear her outlining the best course of action, the importance of saving what few teeth I have, and the cost of a root canal, a permanent crown, and a bridge. I listen politely and nod my head, but I know before she finishes talking that I will opt for having it extracted. Options cost money. Having choices is a luxury we can't afford right now.

When We Gather in Pain

Two weeks earlier

I stumble into the ER clutching the side of my mouth as if my hand were scaffolding holding my face in place. The triage nurse takes my vitals and plugs my information into the computer, telling me to take a seat.

I sit and wait. The waiting room smells sterile, filling my nostrils with the scent of industrial-strength cleaner and rubbing alcohol. I am instantly transported to childhood. I hate hospitals. As I said earlier, I have spent so much of my life in them. For many of us, our stories begin and end here. We are born into weakness and we die in weakness, but in the space between, we spend an inordinate amount of our time, money, and energy fighting, masking, numbing, or pretending not to have any. But I can't mask mine. I hurt too much to pretend.

A woman sits hunched over in a wheelchair, head tipped forward as if she is in prayer. Every few minutes she lifts a tissue to her lips, coughing and dabbing at her mouth. Her hand is dotted with age spots the color of weak tea and traversed with blue veins that seem to knot like tangled yarn under her papery skin. She is all alone, no children or care worker by her side. I wonder how she got to the ER. She lifts her eyes to mine and her lips part in the smallest smile. We both know that waiting to be seen can be the loneliest time of all. We all want to be seen, don't we? Sometimes just being seen and understood is the first step to easing the pain.

The sliding doors glide open and a boy who is all limbs and elbows enters, grabs a wheelchair and wheels it out to the waiting taxi. I see him bend forward and extend his arm like a prince in a Disney movie. Only what emerges is no fairy tale. A woman leans out of the cab, clutching at his arm like she's drowning and he's a branch on the banks to snatch on to. Her last hope before going under. He lowers her into the wheelchair and her face grimaces in pain. She leans heavily against the side of the wheelchair as he pushes her toward the nurses' station.

He doesn't look up or around, his eyes stay focused on the top of her head. He looks as tired as a lifetime of hard could ever look. He's doing man's work. Caring for his mother. Her skin is sallow and sunken, partially hidden under her blue surgical mask, and her voice rasps in agony as she moans.

The nurse motions the boy to wheel her toward a set of chairs with patients waiting to be admitted. She'll have to wait her turn.

After a few minutes, I hear the woman wail, "I've been waiting for a long time! Get me in to see the doctor! I hope none of you jerks ever get cancer and have to know how this feels! . . . Oh, I don't want to hear it! Just get me in, you stupid nurse. Get me in! I can't handle this chemo, you don't understand. I'm dying! I can't wait for your stupid list, I need to go in now! I used up all my pain meds and I need more. I need them now. Do your job, you stupid . . ." Her voice trails off into choice expletives and then fades to whimpers.

She is half crying and half squirming out of her skin as the nurse takes on a clipped, irritated tone and tries to calm her. The nurse is professional but dismissive. At first her voice was soothing like she was talking to a child or an imbecile. But as the rants continue, she is brisk, speaking in short, staccato bursts.

The woman bristles at the slightest touch and her cries echo through the waiting room. When the nurse tries to get a blood pressure, the woman's son helps her peel the layers of clothes off and what's left has been reduced to a body no bigger than a child. She is agony encased in bones and skin and all of it is being poured out, brandished like a weapon, like a lifeline, like a curse.

The security guard comes out of her office and hovers near the reception area. When they've shuffled the woman off behind the doors, I see the nurse mouth to the officer, "Junkie."

"Today it's one thing, tomorrow it'll be something else. That poor kid of hers, though," the security guard whispers as she shakes her head.

My eyes connect with another elderly woman seated near me. She has an Ace bandage wrapped tightly around her ankle and she lifts her eyebrows in disapproval and rolls her eyes when the woman is wheeled across the hall, her mouth pinched disdainfully so that tiny lines feather out from her lips like cracks in dried clay. But the wailing woman is beyond restraint. Her torment is unleashed as she screeches like a siren down the hall, her son trudging after her.

She is flailing and lost and I ache for her. I want to gather her and her son. I want to sit with them. Instead, I do the only thing I can. I pray. I pray into the void, into the pain, into the trauma and poverty that would bring a woman here in the middle of the night rather than to an oncologist's office where she might be treated as a patient instead of as a problem. I don't know if she's battling an addiction or if she's just in so much need that it comes out as vulgar and coarse, but I know what it's like to hurt so bad all I wanted was to be numb, to be nothing. I remember my teen years when my only relief came from the hazy in-between that drugs provided. It doesn't matter if she's an addict or not, at this moment, she's human and hurting, and I feel her sorrow echo in my soul like déjà vu.

I don't know where she's poor, but I know she is. I know it's poverty of soul or poverty of spirit or poverty of circumstance, because this kind of deficit shows. It can't even hide itself and pretend because the void swallows everything. People turn away because it's indecent to be so desperately needy.

We are a society that despises lack. We despise weakness and need and insufficiency. We turn the other way and pretend to be watching oncoming traffic when the red light halts us and the beggar reaches out toward our car with his cardboard sign. We admire pain only if it's healed, only if it's endured with perfect grace, with perfect faith, and never succumbed to in weakness, in f-bombs and rants and curses raised to the heavens.

We gather in pain. We come with wounds and worries, afflicted beyond the scope of our first-aid kit and our Tylenol. We come for healing or at the very least for hope. We come for rest and relief, for remedy.

I pray into the space where we're gathered for this moment. I don't know one word of her story other than she hurts. I know that. I know what it feels like to hurt. And maybe that's enough.

I am in anguish over a few lost nights' sleep and pain too much for me to handle. I am tired and discouraged, trying to survive the radiating ache throughout my neck and chest and jaw, pulsating like a beacon guiding my nerves to battle.

I am crying now. Not a delicate stray tear but weeping violently. Tears are streaming down my face and I don't know where my pain has ended and others' pain has begun, but I know everyone comes broken. The elderly woman rises and hobbles across the waiting room away from me; I have become offensive too. We often become offensive to respectable types when we enter into other people's suffering and brokenness, or divulge our own.

Will I Be Seen?

Tucked behind the curtain in the ER cubicle, I pull the weathered blue gown closed in the back and climb up onto the starchy white sheet.

The nurse enters with my chart and asks me what I'm being seen for, and I begin to explain how the pain started and where. When he finishes typing my information into the computer, he asks my pain level. I tell him it's a 10 out of 10. He taps my veins with gloved fingers and swabs me with the cool sting of alcohol before filling vials to send off. Another nurse tells me the doctor will be back in soon and leaves without ever looking me in the eyes. I wait.

I brace myself for what's coming. I know before the curtain is ever pulled back that I must prove my pain. Before I finally acquiesced to the pleas of my family to get help, I leaned in close to the mirror at home and inspected my mouth, open wide, seeing nothing obviously wrong with my tooth. I applied makeup like I was going somewhere important. I made sure to brush out the mats in my hair from tossing back and forth all through the night. My husband once questioned why I'd bother when I'm just going to the doctor. But I always do when I need to ask for help.

When I have errands like returning something to a store, or asking for a discount, or knowing I will be dealing with someone and their perceptions of me, I dress up. Over time, I have learned it's easier to get help if you look like you don't really need it.

Stores were happy to accept the expired coupon from the elegant-looking white woman with her arms full of shopping bags in front of us in line but were less inclined to do so for my mom, who was missing her front tooth at the time and who bought her clothes from Goodwill.

But none of that effort matters, because I have cried off all of my makeup in the hours waiting and my eyes are swollen and blurry, crisscrossed with tiny red veins like an atlas of my world, marking where I am, how I am, what I feel. This is the nakedness of need.

I wish I didn't have to wonder how I would be treated if I didn't have state insurance, the kind you qualify for when you haven't made enough to buy the real kind. When you have to jump through hoops to see a specialist or get something covered. When a few months of good pay means fewer cutoff notices but your insurance is canceled because you make just a little too much to be considered poor enough. When the in-between of being uninsured means you pray no one gets hurt and nothing happens you can't fix with your medicine cabinet and some WebMD. When you instead learn to live with whatever goes wrong until you can't anymore. When you don't have a primary care physician because you only go in for emergencies. When you get teeth pulled because you have no other choice.

I wish I wasn't stripped of my identity in this gaping hospital gown, with no makeup and bed head, and I could make them see me as a person. I wish I didn't have to wonder if classism or racism was a factor in my care. But I've been dismissed so often, having to prove that I am what I say I am: hurting. I watch the clock tick mercilessly on through the night, counting the ceiling tiles while I pray for someone to see me. To really see me.

Painkillers

I hold my breath for the count of three and feel the dye flushing my veins and rising through my neck, making my cheeks red and hot as the CT scan closes around me like a casket. I'm wheeled back to the ER to await my results.

When the doctor and nurse enter with my scan results, their demeanor has changed. They're gentle, helpfully explaining that the scan showed an abnormal abscess that had broken through my top gum line and, if not treated, would continue spreading toward my brain. Suddenly my phantom pain is justified, and instead of frowning at me as if I am a child faking a tummy ache to get out of school, their eyes show concern and care. My pain is now justified because I have a raging infection pressing on my nerves, and in that moment, I know they finally see me. Strong pain meds are ordered, and the nurse hangs a bag of antibiotics and hooks it to my IV. He looks me in the eyes when he asks gently if I'd like some water and promises me pain relief is on its way. When he takes my IV to administer the pain medicine, he pats my arm compassionately. "You'll feel better very soon," he assures me. The world becomes watery and soft, and my hands drop to my side as my limbs uncoil. Being seen and understood goes a long way toward killing the pain.

To believe that the experiences we have are valid, that the feelings and expressions of them are true and real and worthy of being listened to, is one of the greatest mercies we offer each other.

Poor Teeth

I am thirty-nine years old. Most every picture taken of me, I'm smiling at the camera with my lips closed like I'm holding in a secret. When I go to restaurants, I'm careful to only order things I'm able to chew with my front teeth and my one set of connecting molars.

Nothing indicates your station in life more than poor teeth. The poor don't go to the dentist until their brittle teeth shatter like porcelain, leaving them with a jaw full of rubble. Even then, most dentists don't take random people who can afford little more than a fragment of what's due.

And when I've sat in the dentist's chair, I've often been met with disdain and judgment when the mottled X-ray is slapped onto the light box displaying all the ways I've failed in basic hygiene and discipline. To fix each tooth would be hundreds if not thousands of dollars, and so they are plucked one by one like roots from the earth. There's a reason we use the expression "it's like pulling teeth" to describe something that is difficult and no one wants to do. So I sit, mouth agape, waiting for the void, the empty spot where my phantom tooth can still be felt and where my tongue can't stop probing its grave. This empty and cavernous vacancy spreads in the whole of me. When they look at my chart, I know what they see.

So often when dentists see low-income patients, there is no accounting for the genetics and maternal care afforded to their moms or whether she got prenatal vitamins and enough milk. They don't see a mouthful of teeth competing for space and no money for braces. They don't consider the poverty that would provide a poor diet or food deserts that don't provide nutritious choices. They don't think about access to clean water and the alternative beverages people drink when it's not available. The absence of regular cleanings is viewed more as a failure in prioritizing and scheduling than a maintenance that would mean not paying rent that month. They don't account for constant toothaches that are ignored or old toothbrushes with the bristles worn down and splayed open like the head of a straw broom. No one considers dental floss a luxury and chewing without pain a fantasy. When they look down at the chart and let out a frustrated sigh, they're not accounting for anything other than a moral failure on the patient's part. The disgust that anyone would let it get this bad is palpable.

If you want to make a character on screen insidious, laughable, stupid, or ridiculous, give them snaggled yellow or decaying teeth, give them the stumps worn down to gums or gaps in the front and the audience will fill in the rest. They'll know just what to think.

Sometimes it's easier to keep your mouth shut than bear the shame.

There are many secrets the poor keep, if they can. Keeping their lips shut when smiling is just one of them.

The Poor Can't Choose

One of the biggest distinctions between the rich and the poor is not account balances or stock options, it's choices. The poor cannot choose.

In lean times, we've struggled to pay rent, to buy food, to put gas in the tank, to pay medical bills. For much of my life, we've been one paycheck away from being homeless, and indeed if it weren't for my in-laws letting us move in with them, we probably would've been at one point when the housing market crashed and there was no work. Yet, compared to so many, we are affluent. Now, we're often broke but no longer poor. Our income has fluctuated greatly over the years because of the housing market and the effects it's had on construction, but when you've lived on the sparse side of things for so long, you never forget how it feels to have no options.

I'd lived so much of my life with scarcity a constant companion. Those feelings that God was not going to provide or come through for me is my Achilles' heel. It is my weak spot, the tender area where Jesus asks me to trust him again and again. To walk forward anyway and to believe that in these areas where there never seemed to be enough, he is.

I'd learned to set my sights lower. Always lower. As a newlywed, I'd underline the portions of the Bible that talk about contentment and suffering and I'd hope for the payoff one day. But really, I wasn't so much hoping for character and perseverance as I was for another ten bucks so I could buy some Top Ramen and toilet paper. I was praying for a few extra hours on Josh's paycheck so I could get a winter coat and also make rent that month. I prayed for money to be able to fill prescriptions or go to the doctor when I knew I wasn't well but had no options available to find out why.

I see people who've chosen to live among the poor and are applauded for their noble choices. It's one thing to choose to be among the poor; it's another to not have enough to keep the electricity on or worry your paycheck isn't enough to buy groceries. There's no nobility in that. No one applauds your character when you always come up short.

No one thinks you have succeeded when you have SNAP benefits or you're sorting your boxes of approved cereal and gallons of milk from WIC and trying to match them up to your checks and the worn pamphlet telling you exactly what you can and cannot have, and you can see people looking at your children, appraising your situation, appraising you. Are you a good mom? Are your children well behaved?

Heaven forbid you're shopping at naptime because it's the only time you can walk to the store without it being too hot, and your child throws the expected missed-nap tantrum. Do you look destitute enough? Not too uppity like you're scamming the system, just someone who's fallen on hard times. Or do you look too poor or too fat or too exhausted? So they think you're a lazy slob, just wanting a handout. No one thinks it's great to show up to the church potluck with ramen noodles or one serving of Kraft boxed mac and cheese because that's all you have to spare.

So we learn early on that lack is embarrassing. Our pain is uncomfortable not just for ourselves but for those around us. Our need is obscene and offensive to a world that prides itself on its self-reliance and wide-open smiles. A world where we easily dismiss pain we do not ourselves feel.

Poverty as a Pastor

Being poor doesn't automatically make someone righteous or holy any more than being rich does. But limited material resources, while embarrassing in our self-sufficient society, can create a deeper faith and dependency on God because you don't have the power to do it in your own strength. We know this in theory, and yet we hate being reliant on anyone or anything. We love the power we feel in choice. We say God is all we need but we don't live like it.

As Christians, we must develop muscle memory, the rebounding shape of our spiritual fibers, snapping back into place and getting stronger when stretched further than we've gone before. So many of us let faith atrophy because we don't truly know God's character. We've never had to completely rely on it and therefore can't trust he is good. We lack stamina to walk the long, steep, narrow path we're often called to. It's easy to say God is good when we're #blessed. We associate God's favor with a clean bill of health, a flush bank account, and the ability to bless others. We don't believe our ability to bless others might result from our poverty. Our need might be the thing that most blesses the body of Christ.

Sometimes faith is easier in the crisis. We cry out to God so easily in our desperation—in the storms, the waves, the torrential downpour. The frailty of our condition, our humanity small and powerless in light of the crushing weight bearing down from all sides, is revealed in our inability to ransom ourselves. In the words of one of my favorite hymns, "Rock of Ages," "Nothing in my hand I bring, simply to Thy cross I cling; naked, come to Thee for dress; helpless, look to Thee for grace."[1] There is a helplessness in poverty that precedes the move of God in our lives because we understand an aspect of grace that so many miss: we do nothing to earn it. When we understand this, all becomes grace.

No Shortcuts to Faith

Our suffering works on our behalf when we are powerless, and this is easier to endure for short sprints of pain. But when it is drawn out, a marathon of crisis that becomes our whole life, we begin to look for shortcuts, for ways to anesthetize the pain. We rarely develop stamina in our faith when there are other routes available, as avoiding complete dependence has been our default since Eden. The rich and affluent simply have more options, other socially acceptable routes they can choose.

Christians talk a lot about how we're "blessed to be a blessing." We understand how poor people benefit from the benevolent rich. If we're faithful, we practice generosity. We're reminded of the ways the poor need the affluent to help meet their needs through compassionate charity. We write checks and put money in the offering tray and we take that mission trip but we remain distant. It remains a choice. Our choice. Poverty is something removed from many of us. We often see well-meaning Christians return home from short-term mission trips from poverty-stricken countries gushing about how happy the people there were with so little. How faithful, how inspiring! We send our unruly teens to build houses and get their hands dirty for a week with their matching ministry T-shirts. We hope it will transform them from ungrateful consumers to faithful stewards of all the blessings they have. It will open their eyes to how those other people live and they will feel a small burden to be grateful for their old second-generation iPod when everyone has the latest upgrade.

We return home vowing to be grateful with less; we feel guilty about our Target trips and we skip our Starbucks latte once a week and instead sponsor a child. We might give up some of our excess, but it doesn't really cost us. We become practiced at charity but we don't identify with that poverty internally. Poverty remains foreign, across continents, across oceans, across borders. It doesn't live in our neighborhoods, our churches, our relationships, our homes, and our hearts.

Charity alone allows us to remain distant, and the recipients of our offering are like a specimen to be examined and Instagrammed, a letter or updated picture to pin under the fridge magnet rather than a transformational relationship that would help us know the heart of Jesus in ways nothing else does. Jesus knew that proximity to the poor would transform us. I don't want to discount this. But even more so, he knew putting himself incarnationally into the position of interdependence would be the only way to truly demonstrate the kingdom of God. Indeed, it is the only way we can experience it. We cannot know the inheritance of God without identifying with the poor in spirit, without the poverty that says, "I am naked and poor and wretched and I need a Savior or I'll die. I'm desperate for you, Jesus."

We've valued one side of the equation and not the other because we don't imagine the poor have anything to teach us about God. We go with our gospel but don't always understand grace. We are not students of the poor, the weak, the broken, the outside, or the other. We don't learn from the margins, we still esteem power and success and skill.

What happens when our pastor is poverty? What happens when we are discipled by our lack instead of disciplined for it?

We have merit-based ideology so ingrained into our cultural identity and theology that we often fail to see the great imbalances Jesus constantly pointed out. Much to the irritation of the respectable religious people, Jesus was always elevating the poor and the weak. He knew something we so often forget: none are worthy, not one. Our works are filthy, our hearts desperately wicked, and our lips unclean. And yet, God chose these weak vessels to demonstrate his glory, his mercy, his majesty. He calls us holy, beloved, good, sons and daughters. "For you know the grace of our Lord Jesus Christ, that though he was rich, yet for your sake he became poor, so that you through his poverty might become rich" (2 Cor. 8:9 NIV).

Jesus displaced himself that we might know him. This is incarnational ministry, and it's the life we're all called to. Jesus said, "Blessed are the poor in spirit, for theirs is the kingdom of heaven" (Matt. 5:3 NIV). The word *poor* here isn't referring only to material poverty like the widow in the temple. It's another word, the Greek word *ptochos*, that describes a beggarliness. It means being completely destitute of any wealth, resources, position, skill, influence, or honor. It is a helpless dependence that knows in itself, it is powerless, weak, naked, and empty. It literally translates to "beggarly." It connotes nothing to fall back on. No other route, no shortcuts. No reputation to vouch for you or safety net to catch you because the bottom has already fallen out. This kind of poverty means no choices. And yet Jesus is saying that to come to him, the very first qualification is our realization and identification of our spiritual poverty. Our identification with something so many of us would rather avoid.

By identifying with the poverty in us and around us, we become rich. Yet so often, we don't believe we have anything to learn from the poor.

We think, *Haven't they made the choices that got them into that mess in the first place?* We don't place value on neediness and poverty. There are no accolades for our lack and our weakness. No best-life awards for those who continually struggle. But God places tremendous value there. Throughout the Bible, God spoke of the various reasons for poverty, and while the foolish choices of a sinful lifestyle can contribute to being impoverished, Jesus spent much more time rebuking the affluent for their sinful lifestyles of oppression, greed, and systemic injustice that showed they didn't love, care for, or see their poor neighbors. That, in fact, created much of the inequity that kept their brothers and sisters in poverty. His heart of compassion always bent toward those suffering under the burdens of injustice, poverty, and calamity. Jesus has a decided preference for the weak.

He commanded his disciples to feed the poor, offer drink to the thirsty, and clothe the naked and needy. He told them to practice hospitality to the foreigner. To love the refugees and the immigrants. To nurse the sick and to sit with their pain, to visit those incarcerated and see them as made in the image of God. Jesus adored those we so easily dismiss, despise, or denigrate.

Jesus always taught that he himself was present not only with the poor but also in the poor. Understanding Jesus's presence and incarnational approach to loving our neighbor will always have more to do with identification of our own areas of poverty than with a posture of thinking we're in any way the savior the poor need. The place of blessing we give from is our understanding that all is grace and everything belongs to God. We didn't earn a single thing, material or spiritual. Grace levels us and humbles us to see our neighbor as ourselves. It frees our hands to give and guards our hearts from greed and self-gratification.

In Matthew 25 Jesus taught us that when we fail to see him in the poverty and oppression of others, when we ignore their plight, we fail to understand the heart of God. He made no qualifications of those who deserved grace and mercy. He didn't mention their choices, their gender, their mental stability, their religion, their political affiliations, their country of origin, their work habits, addictions, vices, sins, or the color of their skin. He didn't say to only visit those incarcerated if they were innocent and to limit our love for immigrants to those from Norway, who are gainfully employed and not a perceived drain on the economy. He said in seeing the least of these, in serving them, we would serve him. We would see him. When we begin to do this, displacing ourselves while loving and caring for people who are marginalized, our love has less to do with charity and everything to do with the incarnation of Christ who made himself poor, just for us.

Two

The Ransom of Words

The Glorious Weakness of Longing

We tell ourselves stories in order to live.

JOAN DIDION

My parents' dream of living a life of simplicity, faith, and adventure as missionaries in Nepal ended abruptly the day we found out I had acute lymphoblastic leukemia. My father and brother were up in a remote village when I became listless and fevered. By the time they returned, my mom already had the bad news of my diagnosis waiting and we had a mere day to say our goodbyes, pack our things, and get on a plane to Holland, leaving our home in Nepal immediately to seek medical care not available there.

In the children's ward of the hospital in Holland, the diagnosis of leukemia was confirmed, and they told my parents I might die.

My tiny frame shrunk and the fabric of my skin blossomed with broken petechiae, like tiny redbuds bruising my trunk and slowly fading to muddy yellows and the dull brown of dying blood.

Little Styrofoam statues lined the rolling trays beside hospital beds much too large for the fragile, bare-headed children they contained. Those wig stands stood guard over death, watching with smooth, featureless apathy.

My mother's voice was the song of tranquility in a sea of needle pricks and fluorescent lighting, amid the squeak of sturdy white shoes on cold tile floors as nurses came for me in the dark of night and lifted my weightless wrist to match my plastic hospital bracelet to their chart of orders. The door cracked open like the yawning of a monster's jaw and the flash from the hall would flood the room in a perfect wedged patch of light.

The hush of my mother's hymns provided solace and escape for a girl who couldn't see the light past her own shadow.

In my dying days, my mom's arms were ever present, enveloping me before I even rolled toward her in pain. Her competent hands swam through my baby-fine hair and her trembling voice softly sang,

> Far away in the depths of my spirit tonight
> Rolls a melody sweeter than psalm;
> In celestial-like strains it unceasingly falls
> O'er my soul like an infinite calm.
>
> Peace! Peace! wonderful peace,
> Coming down from the Father above;
> Sweep over my spirit forever, I pray,
> In fathomless billows of love.[1]

Facing Down Death

When I grew up and had survived, we talked about those times, and she spoke of the peace God gave her in that treacherous and trying season. As a mother myself, I can't fathom my child facing life-threatening illness. Would I be able to trust God? Could I surrender to the liminal space between life and death and continue to hope? She wasn't in denial of how bad the situation was and she had zero certainty I would live; instead, those lyrics prophesied peace to her broken heart, no matter what the outcome. My mom arrived at a place in her spirit during those hospital nights where she was able to say, "Yes Lord, if this is your will. I will trust you." My mother, who worries and frets about the funniest little things, who we joke has a forever furrowed brow, startles easily, and never sits still. And yet, to this day, she is the most faithful woman I know. Her trust in God is a testament to how many storms she's walked through, clinging to nothing but Jesus.

Where the Shadows Dwell

My mom saved the books of my childhood. Even when we moved continents, frantically throwing our few belongings into our suitcases, grabbing our family's four passports and climbing on the first available plane, she brought them. We left everything else we couldn't fit in our suitcases, but she made room for the books.

When I was discharged, those books flew with me back to our home in Hawaii where the *lilikoi* fruit burdened the branches of our backyard vines and the trade winds cooled off the blister of the day, chasing off the muggy heat and blanketing us in air as light and silky as mermaid's hair. At night, after the books were read, I would fall asleep only to find my limbs jerking me awake from the dreams, my heart thumping like I had been charged with a thousand volts of electricity, my hair soggy and matted to my forehead. By morning I had always crawled to my parents' bed, where I would collapse right between them into the soundest of sleep. I had already learned not to be alone with the shadows.

At that time, I didn't know we lived in a poor neighborhood, but I knew that the neighbor kids always wore the same T-shirt with the tiny holes day after day while going barefoot, and that everyone's lanai sagged with termite rot.

There was a man named Joey who lived down the road, and every day he would shuffle down to the end of the street and back, staring vacantly ahead while mumbling to himself. It was a ritual to watch his torturous march, and all of us kids made up stories about him, peering quizzically at his slow left foot dragging the loose gravel behind him. He was our very own Boo Radley. Years later, I would learn he had gotten that way from getting high by huffing glue. His parents kept watch over him, because he had lost his mind and the ability he once had to function on his own. At that time, I didn't know people could lose their minds. I would learn that later.

I didn't notice the chipping paint or pipes that rattled the splintered siding on our house. I had never had my own room and didn't know other people did. I didn't register the cockroaches or the termites or the car that kept breaking down as anything abnormal. We all lived like this.

I had seen the rice fields sway in the wind under the shoulders of Annapurna and mothers bundle their babies to their backs, bending and plunging their hands into the water over and over all day long. I had seen the sunken-eyed beggar kids trailing along behind the white foreigners in Kathmandu, palms outstretched as they cried out for pocket change.

I didn't know our house in Hawaii was old and rotten, like the spoiled fruit that fell in our yard and was left to decay on our lawn. My only memory of the narrow hall that led to the bedrooms was the time we gathered all the pillows and blankets from the whole house and stacked them up until they were at my shoulders. My brother and I took turns climbing up on the pile and jumping around. I never saw the ugly and broken around me then, I only recognized it when I looked solemnly at myself in the mirror and cringed at my reflection. Poverty wasn't a novelty; it wasn't something foreign or mysterious. It simply was. I didn't think myself immune to it or above it because I didn't think of it at all.

Longing to Erase Death

In the evening, my mother would stir chocolate pudding mix into warm milk on the stove and swirl it until it set, spooning out a portion for me. She'd set a soft-boiled egg into a tiny cup resembling a shrunken goblet. She'd scoop out the gooey golden yolk with a delicate teaspoon and spread it on hot buttered toast. Food is the way Asian mothers love their children.

I ate what was offered but my mouth remembered dahl and rice and spicy curry rattling away in a pressure cooker, the main staples of our time in Nepal. I remembered scooping hot handfuls into my mouth with my fingers. My tongue had memorized the oil that coated the sizzling fried momos cooked in a large black metal pan on the open flames outside of the Hungry Eye restaurant in the Nepali village we lived in. On special occasions, I'd walk hand in hand with my dad down to the edge of the lake and he'd catch up with our neighbors while we waited for our momos. I learned to bite into them with the tips of my teeth and my lips curled back like a growling dog, to avoid scalding all my taste buds.

But in Hawaii, my mom made fattening me up her top priority. I think she believed it would erase the reminder etched on my bones of those times during my sickness she'd had to face the fact that sometimes God takes away and there's not a single thing we can do about it.

Is God Enough?

Sometimes there are no easy answers. Sometimes God sifts us like wheat and the trials we face are incomprehensible. Is this the hand of God on the threshing floor, in the fire, holding us under the waves, or is this the devil's pythonic stranglehold wreaking havoc while plundering this fallen world? Is it all some random algorithm, some cosmically cruel joke or chance circumstance like a slot machine with more bad luck than wins? If you go big and invest more or start out with a pocketful of shiny gold coins, is the payout bigger, or is the loss more acute? Sometimes faith feels like playing the odds and taking a gamble, and in our darkest moments we fear we are all fools and addicts bowing before a benevolent God who inexplicably also allows mothers to weep over their children's graves.

We wonder: Is God in control, or is he sitting back enacting plan B when it all goes wrong, constantly rerouting us the way Siri calmly chirps directions after we've missed the on-ramp? Which is a better version? A God who is in control but allows or even causes suffering for our growth and his glory, or a God who plays defense—rebounding from our wayward ways and errant choices? A God who is just as dumbfounded as we are when things go wrong but bears no responsibility for the suffering we endure? A God who is a cruel taskmaster, hurling down trials like lightning bolts and checking off boxes depending on how we bob and weave? However you've made sense of God during suffering, we all wonder, Is it enough? Is God enough? Maybe God is neither of these caricatures our minds have cobbled together?

During suffering, we wonder if our faith can save us. And if it can, what does it look like to hold our dying child in our arms and bear witness to a fierce and mighty God who promises he can be known but not always understood?

What does it mean to become foolishness, to confound the wise? To become weak to shame the strong (1 Cor. 1:27)? To be broken in order to be used? To trust even when trusting seems like the stupidest option of all?

How then do we pray? Do we ask for deliverance and mercy? Do we ask only for strength to endure? Do we fall to our knees and thank God for the brokenness, banking on the return abundance? Do we confess sometimes it's so hard to believe?

I don't claim to have all the answers, but I have come to know God is with me. Is he the hand that ransoms me, or is he the hand that crushes me? Might he be both? And if so, how can we retain that God is good?

Indeed, the goodness of God in the face of suffering is one of the eternal questions. It's left people in terror that God may be no better than us. Petty and irrational, sovereign but not compassionate, kind but impotent, withdrawn and passive aggressive.

Wrestling with the aftermath of a child on the brink of death, and trusting a God mighty enough to pull a dying girl back from the abyss yet knowing full well he might still his hand and let my body fail—these were things my parents couldn't easily dismiss.

Whatever wrestling my mother did with accepting God's will and praying for that will to be a miracle for her only daughter, once I was healing, she made amends with all manner of high-calorie foods.

Longing to Be Set Free

Looking at me now, seeing the bulges gather above my waistband like dough set to rise too long, people might assume I have always struggled with my weight. But I wasn't a fat kid. On the contrary, I was hollowed ribs and lanky limbs for much of my childhood. I was gangly elbows and kneecaps too big for my legs. I was a jawline cut straight and tight like a razor's edge and the wasting that comes from sickness and hospitals and appetites lost.

I don't remember this thinness. I've only ever seen it in pictures looking back. When I faced the mirror, I believed the whisper of the shadows, the hiss of a serpent's tongue dripping lies into my ears. I remembered how my body had betrayed me long before I had gotten sick. I remembered how being a girl could get you attention you never wanted but didn't know how to say no to.

When I walked to school in the mornings, I made sure to lag behind everyone because I feared the size of my shadow.

I didn't want them to see the backs of my thighs or the imaginary bulges I believed gathered on my back where I could pinch nothing but skin. I didn't want my classmates to see me at all. I thought I was fat. I thought I was dirty. I thought I was wretched. I was six.

I felt trapped in a body that couldn't be trusted, and even in girlhood I found ways to escape it. Those traveling books were unpacked in the room my brother and I shared and lined up neatly on our bookshelf next to the Rainbow Brite doll my grandmother had bought me, Talitha Bear, and a couple of My Little Ponies.

I picture the girl I once was, rawboned and fragile, lying on her stomach, feet in the air, chin propped in her tiny hand as she fingered the pages of her favorite book—always dreaming of others' stories so she wouldn't have to live through her own. I wish I could tell her she doesn't need to escape to be set free.

But I didn't know that there was freedom for a girl like me, so my escape, my childhood, the memories of home were poured into those raggedy pages. Some barely held together, their spines cracked and their stories slipping from whatever glue and thread still gripped their brittle words, but I just held them gently in my palms and opened them in my lap like a portal to worlds far better than mine. Worlds where the monsters were slain, the serpents were crushed, and the light always won.

A Book Lover and a Storyteller

My mother is a book lover. She polished off gobs of novels, her nightstand a precariously stacked Jenga tower of paperbacks, dog-eared and worn. She taught me to love language and words and narrative. When she was a young woman, the biographies of Jim Elliot, Amy Carmichael, and Mother Teresa inspired her to idealize a life on the mission field. She also read mysteries and the classics, chick lit and contemporary works. To this day, she can rattle off all sixteen digits of her library card without hesitation, like one would their birthday. She always has a stack of fiction books on reserve for her. She taught me good writing and popular writing are often not one and the same, and she taught me to read for rest, to read for enjoyment, to read for liberation. But unlike our childhood books, she moved through hers without attachment. She is frugal both in temperament and in finances, and space was limited, so her books came borrowed from friends' shelves, from libraries, and from free stacks at garage sales. She cycled through them and then donated or passed them on.

I never saw my mom pause during the day to sit with a book unless she was reading to us. She was constant motion, a list of to-dos, always in service to her children or husband or someone in need.

Reading was her long exhale after she'd been on her feet all day. Long after we'd been tucked in and read our bedtime stories, she'd pour herself into bed and reach for one of those dog-eared paperbacks. A slim ribbon would glow reassuringly under her doorway long into the night. It was the only time I saw my mom take time for herself, time no one else needed or claimed.

Although my mom had no intention of passing on a narrow view of God, her tendency toward service and doing, always up to her elbows in everyone else's needs, taught me that our worth is found in what we have to offer, what we accomplish for God. What we earn. This, coupled with the idealism of those missionary narratives, wove a complicated story of grace for me. This is what I learned it was to be a Christ follower. Always pouring out, always being sacrificed, always being martyred for Jesus. Always taking the scraps from a master's table and being sure to be appropriately self-flagellating. I learned we serve dutifully, but we don't ask for more. We learn contentment. We learn how to settle. We learn how to accept our weakness but never ask for God's strength. How to accept our poverty without expecting provision. We learn to live with the ache of never enough. We pray to God as if we don't know him at all, we live with bastardly longing—because a true child would ask. A true child would crawl right up into God's lap and ask for a better story.

A Language of Hope

My father read also, but his was a thirst for knowledge. He too believed in the power of a good story.

My father was what you would call a self-taught man. He left formal schooling 'round about seventh grade. He was born into oppressive poverty of the physical, emotional, and spiritual nature, but his mind was a wealthy and fertile place despite his circumstances. He was a dirt-poor South Carolina boy whose jaw was filled with a hunger for more than his meager childhood could provide.

His mama was illiterate, and she carried shame-filled words inside her, scrambled-up letters blurring the hard edges of her life. Those words claimed her and named her and kept her hopeless. She had no tools to rewrite what she'd been taught.

Sometimes words are the strongest material available to spin life on our tongues and drape hope over those impoverished and naked chapters of our lives. Words are so simple. Just letters strung together. And yet they shift heaven and earth. They explode galaxies. They held space before we kept time. They have life and death contained in each strand, graced on open palms or piled like a burden.

I can't imagine living in a world where words couldn't speak to me and rewrite my truth, and I suppose my dad couldn't either. I don't know what causes some souls to hunger and ache to know, but he surely did. He wanted to know, or maybe to be known. My dad, the best storyteller I ever knew, taught me from a young age about the power stories held. In his way, he modeled how to capture memories because you never know when they'll come in handy. As a writer, the souvenirs of life are stories, snapshots of bygone times exposed to be processed and developed. He taught me that simple parables speak of deeper things. We can't escape our storytelling souls. We're either whispering them to ourselves or offering them to others. Writers lay hold of that internal life and leave a crack in the door. He taught me that entryway matters. We spend lifetimes learning to articulate our great need, our deepest longing. But as Christians, our native language is hope.

Stories help alleviate our myopic vision and the poverty of self we're all born into. We're all squalling infants with a single-volume story, but we were made for an anthology, each chapter inviting us to a place of being known and seen not just as we are but as we may be. This language of hope invites us to a better story.

So, my dad found a different kind of solace in books. He submerged himself and read his way past his seventh-grade skills and was baptized new. He devoured books as if they could nourish the lost parts of his childhood, as if they could mentor him to manhood—educate the poor right out of his life. And in so many ways, they did. He was searching for something life had yet to provide.

Longing for Home

His seeking eventually left him empty and aching while hitch-hiking along the side of the road in Maui. He was a straggly, long-haired hippie who had drifted like a nomad since leaving home around fourteen. He had fallen in with some older men and gotten arrested for breaking and entering. After some time in a South Carolina jail, he was sent to an uncle in Ohio. It wasn't long until he ran away. From there, he bounced around. He knew nothing of permanence or stability. He stayed in communes and slept on couches. He made friends easily, but he was restless and never stayed anywhere too long. Some nights found him locked up for drugs or petty crime. Others he spent sleeping under rocks in Joshua Tree, working concrete or odd jobs, or freezing in Maupin. After one particularly harsh winter he decided to use all his money to buy a ticket to Maui, where some of his friends were going to open a cafe. He arrived there, had no idea how to find his friends, and ended up sleeping in Baldwin Park on the north shore. He ate coconuts and some under-ripe fruit and had not anticipated the stomach ailments nor the monsoon-like rains that can befall the islands. This was anything but paradise.

In a moment of desperation, strung out, hungry, and drenched, he cried out to God. "God, if there is a God, help me!" He woke the next morning to clear skies, a settled stomach, and no remembrance of his prayer. He decided to hitchhike into Lahaina to try to sell some soapstone carvings he'd made.

Helen Jennings peered over her steering wheel and saw a rangy young man, long blond hair matted and greasy, dirty clothes hanging off his too-skinny body with his thumb up as she drove past him on the highway headed into Lahaina. She was a faithful member of a local Episcopal church, and when she passed him she felt she heard God say, "Turn around, pick him up, he's mine." She had never picked up a hitchhiker before, especially not one who looked so weathered, but she obediently pulled to the side of the road and turned her car back to get him.

"I've got one quick stop up ahead to drop off mail," she said once my dad had climbed in. She ended up pulling her car into a dirt driveway that opened up to a stone chapel and a scattering of old buildings. The sign read TEEN CHALLENGE, MAUI. She parked the car and gathered a bundle of mail. A man somewhere near forty pushed open the screen door of the closest building and stepped down the stairs to greet Helen and collect the mail.

Oroville Sexton had had his own love affair with the needle and knew the inside of a cell's sleepless nights. He took one look at my dad and knew his story like it was his own. He knew what the reflection in the mirror looked like after a hard night and he was seeing that same face in this young hitchhiker. Now the director of Teen Challenge, this uncomplicated man wandered out to greet Helen. They chatted out of earshot for a minute and then Oroville ambled over and leaned into the window of the car where my dad was sitting.

"Hey there, can I talk to you for a sec?" he asked, his voice warm. My dad pushed the door of the car open and followed him. Oroville asked him the kind of questions whose answers always reveal more than the words that make up a reply. "How long you been here? Where ya headed? What are your plans?" They chatted easily. When my dad didn't have any definite answers beyond vague mentions of his friends' elusive cafe, Oroville invited him to stay. It was a Christian center where young people came, some from broken homes, some stranded in Hawaii after chasing the dream of endless sunshine and the perfect high, some addicted and desperate. Oroville and his wife, Billie, ran the center more like a family, with them functioning like surrogate parents to many kids who never knew what it meant to truly belong to someone.

"Lovely meeting you, see you later!" Helen shouted cheerfully as she pulled her car back out onto the highway. My dad watched his ride disappear.

And his talk with Oroville turned to religion and God.

"What do you have to lose? Obviously you've been searching, and it doesn't look like you've found much so far. You say you don't really believe in God or at least not in this God, so why don't you stay and prove once and for all that he's not real?" Oroville asked gently.

My dad decided to stay and play along with their proselytizing, hoping to at least get a good night's sleep and a hot meal. He had heard it all before from church people. When he was released from jail the first time as a boy, he was sent to live with his uncle's family up in Ohio. They claimed to believe in the Bible and attended church, but they were cold, merciless people. Even the ones who pretended to care didn't seem to understand what it was like to live in the real world. He had been freezing and begging on the streets in Northern California, hoping for some money to get something hot to eat, when a couple of guys came out of a nearby restaurant holding their tiny boxes of leftovers wrapped up like gifts. They spotted him, and walked over tentatively.

"Hey brother, would you mind if we prayed for you?" one of them asked. My dad said they could, hoping if he endured their posturing they would offer him some change or their leftovers, but when they had finished a long ceremonious prayer, they patted him warmly with their gloved hands, climbed into their car and drove away. He was cold and hungry and as alone as ever. Christians were the worst.

He knew men with track marks extending the length of both arms, mottling their veins in ropy snarls, who would still offer you a length of couch or a spot on their floor on a cold night. He had known women who went from man to man and whose eyes were vacant and lonely who would gladly ladle an extra cup of soup for whoever showed up as a guest. Sometimes the most lost still know how to find each other. Sometimes the only tenderness they get is the tenderness they give. But Oroville was friendly, and a decent bed and meal was as good an offer as he was going to get since he had no idea if his friends had ever even made it to Hawaii.

My father stayed even though he had no intention of becoming some kind of Jesus freak. But God heard those desperate, forgotten prayers splashed about in the middle of the storm. Sometimes the seeds of faith look like a crack in the door we'd least expect. Sometimes it looks like finding a place to call home and a common language of hope.

Longing to Serve God

God was faithful to remember my father, and God was right when he spoke to Helen Jennings that day; my dad belonged to him. God claimed him long before he had any idea what taking that ride would mean. He read the Bible that was given to him and attended chapel if for nothing else than to argue. He was well-read in world religions, history, and philosophy. He could run circles around simple Christians who constantly fell back on "the Bible tells me so." But this time was different. The Holy Spirit was at work.

Oroville didn't come armed with an arsenal of verses to beat him down, instead he had a quiet peace, gentleness, and a sense of belonging. He knew what it was to find grace—it was as if he knew God. Within months, my dad had come to know Jesus. There was no turning back.

Growing up I remember my dad getting into conversations about theology, philosophy, history, and culture, and he could always hold his own in a room full of educated and degreed people. No one would know he had been an uneducated runaway with a criminal record unless he told you his story. And then you might notice the spider tattoo covering his forearm, the one that only had six ominous black legs, which he had tattooed over and turned into a butterfly when I was in grade school. You might notice the faded, milky blue-green ink on the back of his hand with the letters *Co*. A home tattoo he got as a kid. Someone had started to spell *Coors* but the tattoo was left unfinished when his friend passed out. It remained that way his whole life, a reminder of his humble roots. He would tell me these stories when I was a girl. As I listened with a mixture of

horror and fascination, my father never failed to mesmer-
ize me.

There wasn't a subject he didn't know something about.
But even though he could master us all tossing out the answers to Jeopardy questions, he also had a fire to evangelize,
to spread the good news, to offer the language of hope that
had shown him the way home. Much like my mother, he
believed that meant becoming a missionary.

When I was a girl, my dad was my hero. My mom was
my saint. I didn't know how much people could fail you. I
didn't know that even the most dedicated love can still leave
you lacking.

My parents met the same winter my dad met Jesus. He
was a newly committed Christian, passionate and curious,
and she was a shy and contemplative dorm counselor away
from home for the first time. He was loud and gregarious,
the charismatic optimist who could hold a room with his
stories and who was gifted in preaching and teaching, and
she was the reflective perfectionist who was always behind
the scenes doing the real work of making their life together.
They were two polar ends, as different as could be, but they
both wanted to change the world, they both believed in untethered faith and grand adventure. They both said yes to
God in the only ways they knew how.

My parents had nomadic hearts and idealistic minds. They
traipsed across the world believing the call of God on their
lives to be missionaries and trusted with all their hearts God
would provide. To them, faithfulness meant so much more
than sitting in a pew or saying Sunday prayers. They believed
with a simple faith that what God said was true and that
they were to go into the world and make disciples. The how

wasn't as important. They believed the rapture stories of their day and thought the clock was ticking on the world. Their hearts were to serve and evangelize for the sake of the gospel. They lived with little thought for the future beyond heaven. They didn't have a savings account or health insurance. They didn't have a 401(k) collecting money should they someday grow old, or sick, or tired. There was no plan B should their child get leukemia. They were young and optimistic and they heard the voice of God in the wilderness. They packed their suitcases and left for Youth With A Mission in Holland.

Longing to Stay Fluent in the Language of Hope

I celebrated my first birthday having just arrived in Holland, and within the next few years my parents would travel all over Europe leading various mission teams with me and my older brother in tow. We finally settled down for the long haul in Pokhara, Nepal, much to the dismay of many friends and family back home in Hawaii.

"How can you take little kids out there? Isn't it dangerous? How will you make a living?" But my parents weren't deterred, and God did provide a home and a community and a mission.

When they packed their bags they never had any intention of moving back to America. But I'd seen the jaw of an empty suitcase hungrily gobble up what little things we owned and snap shut on our old life. They didn't know that sometimes God's call home is harder than his command to go. Sometimes entering into a new kingdom looks a lot like forty years in the desert first. Sometimes keeping a language of hope fluent on your tongue with dust in your throat is the hardest thing of all.

Three

A Secondhand God and a Place to Call Home

The Glorious Weakness of Lack

> To crave and to have are as like as a thing and its
> shadow. For when does a berry break upon the
> tongue as sweetly as when one longs to taste it, and
> when is the taste refracted into so many hues and
> savors of ripeness and earth, and when do our senses
> know anything so utterly as when we lack it?
>
> MARILYNNE ROBINSON

Shortly after returning to Hawaii from Nepal, my mom attended a women's Bible study and sat quietly as everyone shared. She's a tiny woman, just a few inches shy of five feet. She's always been deeply private by nature and holds things bundled tight inside her small frame, her mother drilling into her from childhood that you don't air your dirty laundry or bring shame on the family. But someone asked how our family happened to come back from Nepal.

People love the highlight reel of missionary stories but not the simple realities that often accompany them. They want stories of Jesus moving and people getting saved en masse but don't want to wrestle with the complications of a life that is often more mundane than miraculous. No one wants to hear about the necessary discipleship that costs energy and sleep. People want to hear about results. They dismiss the small, almost imperceptible changes of living in community and dedicating your life while admiring the glitzy revivals sweeping through boasting hundreds saved, not realizing that for Hindu regions, "converts" are simply adding a god to the plethora they already worship and those "saved souls" don't mean a thing. People don't want to hear about sickness that takes you out more days than you're standing. They don't want to know about how often missions work is going to the market and boiling water and talking to your neighbor. Day-to-day, ordinary life but with less electricity and running water. They don't want to know how much is simply praying and being present. People don't want to know how much is learning from others and being discipled yourself.

No one wants to hear about the doubts that stalk you when everyone said it wasn't wise and now you are broke with a sick daughter to prove them right. But my mom was exhausted, lonely, and overwhelmed, so she shared about my leukemia diagnosis and the upheaval of dreams, our entire life snatched from us with one sucker punch to the gut. In one long, shaky exhale, she shared about the red-light district in Holland where we stayed when I was released from the hospital because we were essentially homeless. She shared how my older brother was struggling to adjust to a sick and dying sister while his mom and dad were gone so much attending her. She shared about returning to Hawaii and discovering her mother had Alzheimer's disease and would need full-time care also. She shared about financial struggles and the shock that comes after the initial crisis is over but the trauma continues.

She didn't speak of the beach house someone graciously offered us because the burdens were so heavy and my family needed a rest. She didn't mention my brother collecting shells on the beach a few feet from the back lanai, or me, her skeletal and healing girl asleep on the couch while my father was working. She didn't speak of the man who broke in through the kitchen window waving a gun and threatening her, shaming her while she whispered silent prayers that I would stay asleep and my brother wouldn't suddenly walk in. Eventually, he was spooked, yanking the phone from the wall and running off, but he had already scarred her and she carried that multitude of stress and loss and trauma into the room with her that night.

"I know just what you mean," a woman chimed in after my mom shared. "I had a flat tire on the freeway last week and it was so stressful waiting for a tow." My mom's eyes dropped to her lap. There were no more words to be said. It was as though all my mother's battered soul was just passed by, and so she learned not to speak up in groups. She learned not to share our stories because no one understood.

When the Crisis Ends but the Trauma Remains

My parents were recommended to a psychologist who agreed to see them for free and help with some reentry counseling.

They took an inventory of life stresses, and when they passed the results back to him, he scanned the list and asked how it was they were still standing. They had a column full of the top life stressors all experienced within the last few months. A sick child, a terminally ill and elderly parent, a major move, a job loss, a victim of a crime, a major loss of income or stability, current job insecurity, loss of community, and health issues. They didn't talk much about PTSD back then but surely my parents experienced some form of it. They handled the initial trauma with a flinty, clenched-jaw determination, but when the crisis ended and the trials continued unabated, sweeping them up like waves pounding the shore, they were drowning.

Bleeding Out and Passed By

Later, I sat in Sunday school and watched the flannelgraph Samaritan bandaging wounds and hoisting the robbed and beaten man on his donkey. It was commonly assumed we were supposed to be the good Samaritan. The obvious morality lesson was "don't be like those sanctimonious priests who dismiss the wounded." My brother and I nodded solemnly and vowed to be good Christians, but when our family came back, we felt less like the hero or the villain and more like the man assaulted and bleeding out on the side of the road. We felt passed by, battered by the brokenness in ourselves and in the world around us. We had felt the sting of those who crossed to the other side to pass by, who clucked their tongues at our foolishness for being overtaken, for traveling down the wrong road, for not being better equipped to fight off bandits like sickness or sorrow, poverty or weakness.

We were devastated by those in the church who refused to come near because our pain was too raw. And besides, "everyone knows you can't take small children to a third world country without something bad happening." It was as if God couldn't be trusted outside of America.

After my recovery, we left our rickety Hawaii rental home where the branches of the banyan stood guard over the neighbor kids running barefoot along the gravelly street. We could no longer afford to live in Hawaii, and the house we were renting was being sold. And because my grandmother had been diagnosed with Alzheimer's disease, she now needed full-time care. My parents prayed about options but knew I was too weak to return to the mission field overseas. My dad flew to Chicago to see about a particular mission opportunity, but once there knew it wasn't a good fit for us. On the flight home, the man next to him got to talking and told my dad, "You don't want to move to Chicago from Hawaii, it's freezing. You should move somewhere like that, like Albuquerque." He pointed out the airplane window at the vast expanse of desert that was New Mexico.

At the same time, my mom was back in Hawaii and had received a phone call from an elderly couple who used to open their home for Bible studies before my parents were married and who had heard of my illness and our subsequent return from Nepal. They were no longer in Hawaii; they had sold their house and moved to Albuquerque. They were calling because they heard of an employment opportunity that might help our family.

My dad was offered a job sitting in a cubicle with a headset and a list of numbers, selling Bibles on cassette tapes to pastors and church ministries. The job was in Albuquerque,

New Mexico. We pulled out the suitcases and packed our books one more time.

Most of my childhood memories collect at the throat of the Sandia Mountains. I still smell the smoky green chili skins charred black like the back of a whiptail lizard sunning himself in the foothills under the hot desert sun.

As a girl, I believed it was my fault my parents ended up so lost during those desert years. We had to stay out of a developing nation because we still had to be vigilant about my health, so we bought our first and only home in Albuquerque when I was eight years old. It was a boxy beige stucco with a dead front lawn. The widower who sold it to us had chain-smoked for years, sucking down cigarette after cigarette, and the tobacco smoke had soaked into the dingy velvet flocked wallpaper that covered most of the walls. There was a two-car garage we could convert into a space for my grandmother to come live with us. The house was run-down but perfect for our budget. It was a fixer-upper in a middle-class neighborhood with good schools and friendly neighbors.

It was the place I first learned I didn't belong. It was the first place I came face-to-face with all I lacked.

I Do Not See God's Pleasure

I remember the first morning of the Balloon Fiesta, the sky thick and shadowy as my dad lifted me from my bed still tucked in my pajamas and blanket and settled me into the car. I'd wake to warm donuts as we snaked our way through the open desert. I remember the taste of hot chocolate, its tiny dehydrated marshmallows bouncing on the top of my

Styrofoam cup, powdery cocoa clumping up as I stirred. I sat wrapped in a cocoon in the back of our old Land Cruiser, watching the sun ascend and the heavens open up to a sea of hot air balloons. I remember the balloon with Mr. Peanut, always the gentleman with his top hat and monocle, looking down impassively with a sham of a smile from his space in the heavens, just like the face of God.

I remember how I sat upright at church in my Sunday best with the scratchy orange pew fabric itching the backs of my thighs and I heard the preacher speak about good gifts. It finally clicked that God had nothing for me, nothing for us. I listened to the preacher tell me the righteous who live by faith will see God's pleasure and blessing, and I knew these were all lies. Because my parents were the most faithful. Everyone in the pews next to us would leave church with their shiny cars and go to their comfortable homes because they'd stayed in the States and had gone to college and advanced their careers. They weren't fools, like my parents, who believed God would provide. Those people knew a degree, a good job, a savings account, and comprehensive medical insurance were the safety net that wise people put in place before obeying God. Trusting God wasn't anything so foolish as total dependency on him. They didn't have childlike faith that trusted that God would never leave them brokenhearted or discarded after being obedient. They didn't pack up their dying girl while giving thanks to a God who heals, without first questioning a God who would let her get sick in the first place.

So I could not stomach these words. They made no sense to me. My parents were faithful, but I did not see the blessings. I did not see God's pleasure.

I remember the worried look on my parents' faces when the shutoff notices showed up in the mail, and their voices arguing behind their door in hushed tones. I remember telling neighbor friends we were remodeling our front room and that's why we had no furniture in there, even though it remained that way for nine years.

I remember my grandma losing her memory, confused and agitated, wandering off in her house slippers and the polyester nightie that she refused to surrender although it was threadbare and obscenely see-through. I remember our neighbors returning her to us, and the embarrassment I felt shuttling her in and away from the neighbor kids' eyes.

I remember the toll it took on my mom to care for her as my grandma's mind rotted and her memories vanished. There was no peace in that surrender. It was a hostile takeover of myelin and brain matter.

Some days she would remember to ask us how school was, and my brother Jordan and I would dutifully answer her over and over as she forgot that she had already asked, each retelling less detailed until, in our exasperated youth, we yelled, "Grandma, we just told you!" And we would watch her face contort, a horrifying mixture of confusion, terror, and rage.

On the night Grandma died, my mom was worn like a rag that had been wrung dry from pouring out so constantly as only an attendant to the dying can, and she said no to my grandma's requests. "Not now, I'm in the middle of something, I'll come soon," she promised. And later, when my dad checked on her, my grandma had passed peacefully in her sleep. But that "no" would haunt my mom. The dutiful daughter failing at the last battle. *Why that night, Lord?*

Why take her the only night out of a thousand that my mom didn't put my grandma's needs first? Why?

Death blew through the desert like a rolling tumbleweed, and all we heard was the haunted howl of a full-throated coyote, scavenging for bones—or maybe that was us, our collective animal cry, screeching at the moon and cursing God.

When I heard the preacher say these things about blessing, it made no sense—unless we aren't pure and blameless, unless we're not righteous or faithful. If the formula is fixed, then there's no escaping that we've been flummoxed and mishandled our end of the deal. Or God is a liar and a thief, promising blessing but providing pain. In my mind, it could not be both.

I'm the One Lacking

And then I came to know what I'd always felt: it's my fault. I wished I could tell my parents the truth. I'll remember when the door closed behind me and the curtains were pulled tight to the light and I felt my world close in, those dark and smudgy edges burning up my innocence. I'll remember how I looked up to the teenage boy who lived in our missionary community in Nepal. How he was nice to me and would play with me even though I was only four or five. Only that trust broke when he unzipped his pants and pulled out his penis. I squeezed my eyes shut as tight as I could when he tugged gently at my pants and pulled them down and I know that even though my parents couldn't see me, God could. And that makes no sense at all. Because if God can see, why would that happen? So I believe God looked the other way when I felt that boy's fingers pushing into me, guiding my hand to touch him, trying to penetrate me while I squirmed under his grasp, and I'm only just a tiny girl, barely past a toddler but with enough memory so as I can't forget and I let it spoil everything. Those "play times" would terrorize me with memories I couldn't repel. I'll come to believe that is why I was sick and that is why I am poor and that is why I am dirty. That is why my parents can't pay their bills and my grandma is dying and I don't fit anywhere.

The times my family attempted to put down roots and live like the Joneses, we always fell short, next door to the doctor's kid with their brand-new ten-speed and us with our secondhand Huffy with the cracked vinyl banana seat. And this is what I came to believe about God: it doesn't matter how hard you try, how fast your legs pump or your heart beats, how high you lift your hands or how earnestly you pray, some people will never keep up.

Being a secondhand kid in a department-store world can make you start to believe that God only has scraps for you. It'll teach you envy and bitterness if you let it. All you see is what's lacking.

I let it spoil all the good things God had for me. I saw only his castoffs. Nothing will ever be shiny and new and abundant. I faithfully worship the god of scarcity, a stingy and mean god, a secondhand god who is always holding out. A god who turns the other way.

The Great Pretender

I never figured out the right way to stand when we all gathered in youth group. Never knew where to put my hands or what to say. Never knew how to dress or which jokes to laugh at. So I watched.

I developed chameleon flesh, blending as seamlessly as I could into my surroundings, which wasn't easy when you're the only Asian American. I longed to be noticed, and I longed to disappear with equal fervor.

I learned to giggle at the right things and crease my brows together at the appropriate times, looking sufficiently concerned over the grave issues of sin and the wages of death. I scribbled notes in the margins of my NIV Youth Study Bible and dutifully highlighted portions at home so when the pastor called us to turn to a passage my fingers would skim the feathery pages while yellow flashed like a beacon that I was doing it right. I held my Bible down low on my lap so others could see I was one of them. Pious and committed, a Jesus girl who followed the rules and loved God. And I learned to pray hard and earnestly for the lost we were supposed to evangelize while unsure if I was one and the same. I learned to cry heavily weighted sobs at the altar like all the other middle-school girls. I silently repeated salvation prayers over and over like a transaction that kept getting denied because I was already overdrawn, already so greatly lacking.

I must have gotten "saved" a hundred times because I could never be sure if it took. If God was real or if I had just learned to imitate those around me so well that at times I almost felt something. Every shiver or goose bump might be the Holy Spirit, but it also might be the ramped-up air-conditioning in the sanctuary during the sweltering summer months. I'd close my eyes when the worship music swelled. I'd lift my hands, singing, "Our God is an awesome God." I tried my best to believe it. I wanted so badly to believe it, but even as the words came out I couldn't get past my creatureliness reminding me my flesh was all consuming. I wasn't a new creation. I couldn't possibly be, I was still just a girl with a dirty mind and jealous thoughts.

The kids around me always did it better. They had the white-blonde American good looks and their daddies drove fancy cars and had important jobs while their moms stayed home and baked cookies and fixed after-school snacks. I tried taking up less space, so I could fit easily into the life I craved. They made it look so easy.

I'm Other

I teased and back-combed and curled my stick-straight bangs trying to achieve the perfect hairstyle, which most closely resembled a cresting three-inch ocean wave. But even after I emerged from a cloud of Rave hair spray, my hair would sag pitifully. I leaned into the mirror and opened my eyes as wide as they could go, watching my eyebrows lift as I imagined ways to erase the unmistakably Asian-looking girl staring back at me. I longed for deep-folded eyelids, a stretched canvas for blue eye shadow so I could do the makeup tutorials in my friends' *Seventeen* and *YM* magazines. I wanted to be beautiful like teen models Niki and Krissy Taylor. I hated when kids would pull their eyelids back into cruel slits and chant "ching chong China girl," lined up like they were singing carols. I longed for blonde hair and blue eyes and a name like Jennifer or Melissa or Sarah. Teachers would read my name and it would roll around in their mouths like something foreign and wrong before it plopped out. Oll-yah? Uh-lie-uh? I never bothered correcting them. I never found my name on any of the personalized novelty lunchboxes or pencils or mini license plates people had.

I begged for money for pizza or Lunchables even though the crackers were stale and bland and there was always a hunger in me that wasn't quite filled. I didn't tell anyone that home was Spam, saimin, kimchi, and seaweed. That we always had a rice pot plugged in on the counter.

I wore Kmart white sneakers instead of the name-brand Keds. I longed for Guess, Gitano, or Z. Cavaricci jeans so I could roll them at the ankles and tuck them into my slouchy white socks like all the other girls did. My mom did her best to send me to school with an acceptable lunch and to outfit me with clothes I felt comfortable in, but she didn't realize I would never feel comfortable no matter what label I wore. I had already labeled myself. Other. Someone who didn't belong.

A Porsche, Not a Porch

"Not a porch, stupid. A Porsche! Don't you know anything?" She cocked her head to one side, her strawberry-blonde hair falling over her shoulder as she wrinkled her freckled nose in distaste.

I still had no idea what she was talking about. She said her father got a porch. Finally seeing an opening with which I could participate, I proudly stated that we had a front and back porch and the back one even had a porch swing. The clan of third grade girls turned their eyes on me like I was prey for their hungry mouths and wagging tongues, and then suddenly they all erupted in laughter. I stood paralyzed, feeling the color coil through my veins and flush my face a splotchy crimson. I mumbled something about not hearing correctly and retreated to the classroom with their cackles echoing in my wake. That year, I was at a private Christian school, but I was on a financial scholarship. I had no idea what a Porsche was.

No Opening to Belong

I was the girl who stood on the outside of countless circles shuffling my feet inelegantly. This was before the days of cell phones and the ability to cushion the lonely awkwardness with a backlit screen, pretending to text some illusive friend because the girls around you never stepped back a bit to let that circle widen. I would approach tentatively and stand at the edges, dipping my toes into hope, praying to be noticed and invited in. Sometimes I'd rehearse in my mind the words that would gain me entrance, and my heart would pound in my ears and I'd swish my tongue across dry lips and look for an opening to belong. I'd push the words out high and strangled and they'd fall between us and land heavy on the ground, and my eyes would seek refuge in the tangled knots of my shoelaces as they inched back. The blotchy heat would climb from my chest up into my cheeks, and I'd mumble something about needing to be somewhere and their eyes would all slide off me like I was never there at all. I stared at the backs of heads, their stiff shoulders like an impenetrable fortress for the elite, and all I ever saw was the ways I didn't fit. I grasped at conversations like crumbs falling from the table, but each attempt made me look more like the beggar I knew myself to be, and my voice trailing off into silence sounded hollow and ridiculous in my own ears.

Good and Evil

So I stop believing God is good.

At church on Sunday, when the preacher pounds his fist dramatically on the pulpit, I believe those flames are meant for me because I don't know if I am a virgin, and this is the highest aspiration for a middle-school girl. Our virginity is the thing we have to offer back as a gift to God and our future husband, our future children. In youth group, my friends' parents buy them expensive promise rings when they vow to stay pure until marriage, but I am not sure what counts, and I know my parents couldn't afford one anyway. I believe what happened to me when I was a child made me impure. I am pretty sure it is my fault because I never verbally said no. I never said anything at all. I know things I shouldn't know, dirty things, but I want a shiny slip of silver or gold to place on my finger too.

I want to be claimed by a greater love.

At night when I lie in the suffocating darkness and feel as alone as one ever could, I'll believe I only get secondhand things from a poor and mean god because I know the taste of good and evil and my eyes are wide open. Death lingers in my bones. The garden is long gone, we are lost in Albuquerque's desert lands.

I don't yet know our lack leads to God's abundance. Barren places long to be filled. Sometimes howling at the moon in the wastelands with our fists raised to the heavens is our most honest prayer for Jesus to come down from the high and distant places we've relegated him to and walk with us on scorched and humble feet. Sometimes the holiest ground is the emptiest.

Part 2

hope

four

I Am Not Labeled,
I Am Named

The Hope of Identity

Once you label me you negate me.

Søren Kierkegaard

Throughout my life, the voices came for me, and they carried in their whispers the ancient shame, their tongues curled into my ears, trailing me through my day. They hissed that God couldn't have said I was good. They implied that maybe, like so many things, I had gotten this wrong too. And they were always there with reminders of the ways I was damaged goods.

As a child, I swallow the lies politely, like a good girl, instead of spewing them out.

Instead, I succumb to the burden of brutal words. Sometimes it's easier to be what they expect.

As a teen, I morph into the girl stomping onto the front of the stage, black Doc Martens thudding with a heaviness I've learned to conceal.

I'm tired of being good. I'm tired of asking God into my heart and rules I can't keep because despite it all, I know my heart's beat is wicked. I'm tired of the hypocrites trading faces. I am tired of a God who refuses to show his.

Instead, I write poetry in the dark under the blunt-edged light of my Marlboro red. My cigarette butts stack themselves like crooked bones, a graveyard of the hours spent curled around my journal scribbling furiously, carving out my confessions. Every word hurts.

My pages are smoke and cinder, fire and dust. Other people's words scald my tongue and I exhale mouthfuls of ashen syllables.

The voices promise me I'll always be hollow and empty and wretched.

And ever since the day I was called *girl*, they have understood my tender spots. The day the voices first come for me I am five years old and I keep secrets in the dark. I learn unspeakable things happen to little girls. I am groomed by the lethal burden of silence. I walk bruised in tender parts. I learn this identity and wear it with pigtails over ears scalded with shame.

Ghost Girl

I am ribs and skin and sunken eyes for much of my girlhood, a haunted child. I am long, braided hair so thin and wispy, the plastic daisy barrettes slip down no sooner than my mother places them, and I hope to grow ghostlike, an apparition no one can grasp hold of. If I am bodiless, I can escape capture. But I learn a girl's body will betray me all over with the legs of a woman and breasts that draw catcalls and lusty eyes, and I am to blame. I learn I can be violated again and again with unholy tongues.

"She's exotic," they say. "Once you go Asian, you never go Caucasian." They laugh and never see past the slant of my eyes to the vacancy their words leave. "I've got Yellow Fever," they joke, palpating their hands over their hearts as I walk by. Their labels slither serpentine down my hips, all venom and fangs and poison so strong it takes me years to believe myself anything but nasty. I learn I am nothing more than fantasy, than fodder for locker-room talk, than rumors and wagging tongues. Boys will be boys after all.

Exotic. Slut. "We're just joking, you should be flattered. It's a compliment."

Goldilocks and Being Just Right

I contort into a thousand roles depending on who I am around. I try them all out like Goldilocks, co-opting identities trying to find the "just right" fit. And when I fail, I pull on labels others dress me in. I grasp at the threads trying to weave an identity thick enough to cover my nakedness.

He slings his arm lazily around my shoulders and drips his fingers down my collarbone like he's strumming chords on the neck of his guitar. I am hollowed out, percussive and echoing whatever beat they play. I am a girl used to greedy hands, and when I grow from childhood, I am once again prey for hungry eyes, a girl who's been plucked down to bone for the curve of my breasts and the bow of my lips. The kind of girl who always feels hunted. I walk around in borrowed skins.

I was the girl so uncomfortable in her own, she grew more and more until they swallowed her whole.

The Lies Full Grown

And the years pass. I believe the skins will shelter me from carnivorous eyes. My breasts balloon, my belly shakes full of lies, and I'm magic. Maybe now I have achieved invisibility?

I am a new stereotype, a new label. My fat body dictates my identity for me. Society demands I apologize for being a fat woman, for the space I take up, for the choices I make, but it needs no explanation. It knows everything there is to know about me with one look.

I'm a fat woman. I'm not seen as a whole person, because I am a full person and a full person is automatically lazy, slow, undesirable, gross, slobby, out of control, and asexual.

When slim girls eat pizza and joke about pigging out or eating fast food, they're charming and down to earth. They're celebrated for being real and not obsessing over their bodies. But if a fat girl did the same, she'd be criticized for not obsessing more, for not making healthier choices. If a slim girl loves wine and chocolate and carbonara pasta served with crusty artisan bread drizzled in olive oil, she's a foodie. If a fat girl does, she's self-indulgent and lacking willpower.

The church fancies up the language with biblical terms, but they amount to a lot of the same stigma surrounding fat bodies. In church, my fat often determines my gluttony in others' minds with nothing more than a casual glance. Sluggard, slothful, slowly destroying my temple, and lacking self-control to properly discipline my flesh—so much flesh. No one accepts that my fat isn't my greatest sin because it is offensive to take up so much room without repenting of the calories I've claimed and carried on my body. My body is seen as a confession of the ways I've sinned against God. It keeps the equation simple, but it masks what truly grows in me. The shame of an unknown girl.

The same shame that halts another girl's fork before it reaches her lips again and again as the number on the scale plummets, that keeps her cutting the tender flesh of her forearm or her thighs where no prying eyes can judge, the same shame that keeps a girl's body on display like an accessory or in the bed of anyone who says, "I care." The same shame that keeps the credit card sliding and the shopping bags attempting to fill the void. The same shame that keeps the good girl's hands lifted in church for everyone to see and the complicated prayers tumbling from her lips as she tries harder and harder to be loved.

My shadow voices followed me from girlhood and swell like a prophecy, the lies have come full-grown inside me. I have conceived sorrow, reaping my curse.

I stuff myself into bodiless sweatshirts and go barefaced against the world. I drain the color from my eyes and make jokes about myself before anyone else can. I carefully turn off every single light and let the darkness cover me when my husband reaches for me at night. My hair is unwashed, scraped hastily into a ponytail. I can't meet my own eyes, I avoid my reflection because I do not know who that woman is. I've never known. I don't want to be seen. I hate having my picture taken and all the memories I have are blurry photographs, my hand blocking my face like I'm ashamed of being remembered at all.

Sadness becomes my natural habitat. I surrender to the ache of being unknown. And the voices come for me as I grow into motherhood.

When the child crumples in the shopping cart and his face turns mottled and red as his wailing rises from his sobbing little chest, and the shoppers raise their eyebrows and cluck their tongues because I am not doing this right, the voices rush back.

I can hear the faintest hum of "Hmmph, she really ought to discipline that child . . . brat . . . my child would never . . ." and it gets louder until I'm frantically removing Goldfish crackers, and milk, and ground beef, and toilet paper onto the conveyor belt and rifling through my purse for coupons and my debit card while shushing Judah with a mix of embarrassment and frustration. I drop the frozen orange juice and the container splits like it's gutted and the pulpy mess oozes onto the supermarket floor. They call for cleanup on checkout three and the voice on the loudspeaker thunders in my bones. And I stand there in checkout lane three and I feel myself spilling out too. Making a mess everywhere I go. And everyone looks on and they can all see I'm not cut out for this.

The voices come when I gather with other women. These women smile with mouths full of words people want to hear. They toss their heads back when they laugh, deep and throaty—their hands don't fly up instinctively to cover their mouths when they do. They say the right things and people lean in closer. They don't mumble and trail off when people turn their heads mid-sentence, and I drop my eyes to the floor as the voices come for me. *You could just go, no one even wants you here. You are invisible or worse, an annoyance, a burden. They only invited you because they feel sorry for you. You are drama and chaos and they all pity you, if they notice you at all.*

Who Am I?

In the desert, we are introduced to a terrible and mighty doubt. Weaving our fig leaves, we become the great pretenders or we become who we were always meant to be. Unashamed. No one remains unchanged in the wilderness.

I forget Jesus knew the landscape of the desert too. The Spirit led him into the wilderness and directly into contact with his hunger. Creaturely appetites fixate our gnawing dependence on the tangible goods this world has to offer, the things offering sustenance. The void swells in our bodies, reminding us how much we need, how much we lack. But Scripture says that after he had fasted forty days and forty nights, Jesus then became hungry (see Matt. 4:2).

What nourishes us when confronted with doubt in the desert? Jesus knew the voices would come for him just as they do for us. And the tempter came and said to him, "If you are the Son of God . . ." The first attack was on Jesus's identity and relationship with the Father, not on his hunger. "Tell these stones to become bread," followed (Matt. 4:3 NIV). But the great temptation of Jesus started from another front: Are you who you say you are? Is God? Can you trust your Father? Can you meet your own hunger? Can you save yourself? Can you name yourself?

Jesus is tested again on the cross, a posture of complete surrender and weakness. The soldiers mock him: Aren't you the King of the Jews? Aren't you the Christ? Save yourself! Only a fool or an imposter would die instead of ransoming themselves with a thousand angels. It is an assault on the relationship and identity of Jesus.

Can you trust God at your absolute lowest, at your absolute end? Will you take this cup? Will you drink from suffering? Jesus modeled full identity, strength, and power by surrendering to unfathomable weakness, even unto death. But the Son knew his Father and when Satan whispered in his ear, Jesus didn't fall or fly into the heavens, bypassing the cross. Jesus fought back, offering us a ransom of words, the nourishment of "every word that comes from the mouth of God" (Matt. 4:4 NIV). The original language of hope stayed fluent on his tongue.

Jesus knows the voices we face, and his promise to send a Comforter to be with us forever anticipates that our lives will be filled with grief and sorrow, with desert wanderings and our consuming and ever-present weakness. Why would we need a Comforter unless he knew we would be uncomfortable? Unless he knew we would need comforting? Jesus says, "But the Advocate, the Holy Spirit, whom the Father will send in my name, will teach you all things and will remind you of everything I have said to you" (John 14:26 NIV).

Jesus knows we face an accuser; he knows the voice that comes for us. The Holy Spirit is prepared for the grief, sorrow, trials, and accusations common to us all, and we are ministered to by the Spirit of Truth even in the wild—especially in the wild. Jesus knows we will be ravaged by our hunger, by our doubt, by the tendency to want to sustain ourselves, protect ourselves, rescue ourselves, nourish ourselves, name ourselves. He also knows we are utterly incapable of remaining sober minded on our own, not when we face such terrible lies, such loud voices of accusation. Jesus promises we will not go into the wilderness alone. We will not be left hungry. We have a Counselor to defend us. A Comforter to tend to us. We have a language of hope that speaks truth to us and calls us out of the desert, changed forever. "And I will ask the Father, and He will give you another Counselor to be with you forever. He is the Spirit of truth" (John 14:16–17 HCSB).

We Are at War

Sun Tzu said in *The Art of War* that "all warfare is based on deception."[1] The battle for our true selves, the *imago Dei* in us, is assaulted at every turn. Sin has sown discord in our hearts and reaped a bounty of pride, fear, lust, racism, white supremacy, misogyny, xenophobia, sexism, homophobia, ableism, ageism, classism, and so many more spores now flourishing full grown like toxic mold within our atrium and ventricles, pumping deception into our souls. Its nucleus is invisible to our clogged eyes but it is everywhere choking out life, filling our bodies with disease. We don't realize we're colonized, but the symptoms are everywhere. We separate ourselves, we tell ourselves we don't belong or declare that others don't. We become divided instead of diverse. There are countless ways we declare the image of God as not fully present in other people. And when we don't see the image of God in others, we'll fail to see God. The image of God has nothing to do with merit, nothing to do with status, or character, nothing to do with our body's ability or lack thereof. It has everything to do with God's imprint on his most intimate creation. We don't earn it, it is bestowed, incarnate, essential to who we are. Beloved.

We are hardwired for self-deception and self-preservation though. Sometimes we know we're doing it, sometimes we choose it out of habit or comfort, but often we don't. Our subconscious is a mighty adversary, and if you've survived childhood you have learned to self-preserve in one way or another.

I have stared into the solemn brown eyes of my baby still clad in diapers and covered in chocolate from chin to cheek while he's sworn up and down that he did not in fact find Grandma's hidden stash of candy and eat it all. There could be wrappers trailing Hansel and Gretel–like behind him and still he denies truth. I wonder if sometimes God shakes his head at us, with the kind of gentle knowing only a parent could have, and sighs, because don't we know he gets it? Don't we know he would've offered us a treat himself? Don't we know he loves us?

We tell such eloquent lies about who we are, who others are. We masquerade as orphans instead of as the beloved children of God. Deception surely plays a role.

What is the point when these lies began to germinate? What feeds the disease? What nourishes and hides our sin? What perpetuates the grand cover-up? What intoxicates and numbs us? What keeps us from truth?

The lie might be so big the world came undone in a moment. You might have soaked your pillow every night believing you were dirty and could never be made clean. You might have told yourself it was your fault. You might have believed God turns his head the other way, or looks on and simply doesn't give a crap, determined to get you good for the wrong you've done. You might have learned to weaponize your body, your soul, to keep yourself from ever being hurt again. You might have learned to despise your body, wishing away every synapse, every cell, every joint, and decided that punishing yourself by making it disappear, by making it bleed, or by starving it completely was the only way you could deal.

The lie might have been that your life doesn't matter to God, because it surely doesn't matter in the world. You might have watched your skin color be assigned value in the classroom, on the television, in the store every time you feel watchful eyes on your back. You might feel the burden and oppression of your ancestor's market price. You might have been stopped and frisked so many times because others see nothing but a threat, a commodity, a problem. And you always drive with your hands at ten and two but know deep down that keeping them up won't help, you'll never be innocent in your skin.

The lie might be that you have to defend God. That you have to stand up for the truth, and it looks a lot like keeping the riffraff out. You are a card-carrying member of the people of God, the fixers, the get 'er dones, clambering for their place in the hierarchy, in the empire that was never of God. You might believe you can become tainted by the evil in the world if you get too close, without realizing what festers in the fleshiness of your own wicked and desperate heart. You might believe the image of God departed from those sinful ones, with their wayward desires, with their addictions and their perversions, their foul language and their folly. You might believe a prodigal can never come home, still reeking of feces and puke from gutter sleep and orgies and poverty. You might cross your righteous arms in refusal to join the celebration and look on with disdain as God makes a fool of himself running toward his beloved child, with arms outstretched and limbs flailing in pure joy and anticipation—not waiting to first weigh and discern with a calculated coldness what explanation and apology his disgraceful kid has to offer. Is he penitent enough for the wrong he is?

The lies start somewhere. Maybe we have no origin story other than we saw a way to know ourselves apart from God, to make sense of everything, to become our own nourishment, and only after we tasted the seeds of sin, felt the nectar of our choices flowing down our chins sticky and sweet, did we see it was rotten. We invited death and deception into our beautiful world.

That warfare leaves its scars on us, marks us with lies. Lies we tell, lies we are told. Lies we become. Are we arrogant or are we afflicted?

We are not good enough or we are too good. We have no place at the table, no banquet for us, no safe haven—or we are invite-only, RSVP and black tie required. We don't take truthful stock of both the wickedness of our afflicted hearts and also the belovedness of our everlasting souls.

If all warfare is based on deception, truth is the weapon to fight against the lies. The balm for our scars. To flourish in relationship we need a bridge of truth to connect us. The cross is the greatest truth we have. The X on the map, the way home, the treasure unearthed.

The antidote for the voices that come for us is our true identity as beloved. The cross tells us the truth. I don't know of a fiercer love than this: while we were sinners, Christ died for us. We are not shamed or self-satisfied, we are saved. We return to the slippery-tongued serpent and hear the hissing in the whole world, and even though lies come easier, we tell ourselves a new story. We hear the good news.

The Power of True Words

We are hardwired for self-deception and self-preservation, but the Word of God is intrusive. Disruptive. Subversive. It tears at the skins we've hidden ourselves in, and that's agonizing.

The power of true words comes to fruition in repentance. Weakness is seminal to grace. Nothing can be birthed that has not first stretched and ripped you open. Truth is the midwife that helps us labor long and hard during the process.

What I had gotten wrong about my salvation attempts all those times I timidly raised my hand for altar calls was that deep down I only saw my sin and scars. I only saw that I was dirty and separated from God. I only tasted bitter fruit and heard the voices accusing me. I only saw where I didn't belong. I saw my lack, but I didn't see God's abundance. I needed the truth of the gospel. It is the goodness of God that brings us to repentance.

For those who put their trust in God's love, the cross neither condemns nor condones, it only ever covers us with Jesus. This kind of truth is intrusive but it is also redemptive. It both unmasks and covers.

It's the most beautiful truth I know. We are claimed by the devastating love of God's grace. I am claimed by a greater love.

hope

Set Free and Called by Name

The nature of gospel truth is to confront, but its purpose is to set us free. I didn't know when I was filling those journals in my teens that I was crying out to God, because all story-telling is a confession of sorts. I was thrashing about in the dark, reaching for a lifeline.

But Jesus gathers the weary ones, the ones who can no longer hear anything but accusation and despair, the ones whose ears ache in agony and ring with the need for good news. We count ourselves among the poor, the oppressed, the weak, the meek, the wandering, the poor in spirit, the hemorrhaging, the unclean, the broken, the thirsty, the out-cast, and the other because we know Jesus came for just such ones. We know we are more than the labels the world places on us.

And the voice that cancels out all the whispers and the hiss of unholy tongues says, "*I have made you good.*"

Maybe all of life is just a journey back to the heart of God, back to the garden where we saw his face and he called us good. Back to the place where we remember who we are by knowing who he is.

"*Fear not, for I have redeemed you;*
I have called you by name, you are mine."
I am not dirty. I am not what they say. I am not
what was done to me. I am what Jesus did for me.
Redeemed.
"*When you walk through fire*
you shall not be burned,
and the flame shall not consume you."

I can spit out mouthfuls of ash and scalded tongues
are quenched with a language of hope.
These lies have no claim on me.
"For I am the LORD *your God,*
the Holy One of Israel, your Savior."
No longer a lost girl, no longer a label or a stereotype.
Named. Beloved. Ransomed.[2]

My shadow still spreads across the light, but these days it dances to new songs. These days I stand on tippy-toes to kiss my husband as his arm circles around me, pulling me closer. I'm at peace with my body, with my soul, with my identity as beloved.

I pull my swimsuit cover-up over my head and drop it on my beach chair before joining my kids in the water. They swim toward me. My arms, fleshy at the tops like a pair of '80s shoulder pads that have slipped down too far, are the only ones they know. I am familiar. I am known. I tuck my arms around their bodies, pulling them through the water while they squeal with joy. We stay in long enough for our fingertips to wrinkle as we dunk each other or race across the top— the first one to the floaty wins. My body isn't consumed by shame. When the voices come for me, I remember whose I am.

God provides the reminders when I need them. Jesus sees us despite our three-way mirrors and bad lighting, despite the labels we wore or the sizes we fit in or don't. My hands stretch into the summer sun to lift children on those hips and my family calls my body home; I drop my hands and let my picture be taken. I will be remembered.

I am Alia Joy, which means ascending to God's joy. My name, which I long hated as a girl, which I thought made me different when all I wanted to do was fit in, was, in fact, a promise that in the midst of my weakness, the joy of the Lord would be my strength.

These days I'm not hiding. I'm shedding skins and writing my way back to the truth. To the identity I had long forgotten and the place where I remember I am not labeled, I am named.

five

Uncomfortable Love

The Hope of Community

It cannot be denied that too often the weight
of the Christian movement has been on the side
of the strong and the powerful and against the
weak and oppressed—this, despite the gospel.

HOWARD THURMAN

When I was in Albuquerque, church poisoned what little
faith I had left. The boys pretending to be pious in church on
Sunday mornings in the presence of their parents and pastor
were the same ones trying to get in my pants on Friday night,
their boozy breath promising me they really cared. The girls
who showed up for the youth group lock-in were the same
ones huddled together gossiping and making sure the circle
never widened enough for everyone. Much like my father all
those years ago, I thought Christians were the worst.

Lifeless bodies filled pews deadened to anything beyond a sterilized message and some platitudes about being a good Christian, which seemed to boil down to not cussing, drinking, smoking, watching R-rated movies, having premarital sex, being gay, or having an abortion. Achievable morality ruled the day. Nothing too lofty like pride, greed, lust, racism, covetousness, or idolatry. Nothing that would make the respectable Christians uncomfortable or needing to examine their hearts further. Instead, their actions could be weighed and found acceptable as long as they played by the rules. They readily accepted a white middle-class Jesus with flowing golden-brown locks and pearly white teeth who solemnly condoned whatever they did with their lives as long as they were generally good people. After all, look how blessed they were. That must count for something.

Planting Bitterness

My parents' hearts yielded bitter fruit. Because they were cynical idealists, and those traits were fundamentally at odds with each other, the church offered no solace. They grew disillusioned with it all. Even now, it scares me how easily bitterness turns to hate. Hatred kills idealism and cynicism equally. It is an equator to land on. It often begins with lament and justifiable anger, feeling productive and right— godly even. It starts out aimed at iniquity, injustice, and the apathy of God's people. You can't tell me the thought of flipping tables doesn't inspire a lusty, red-blooded thrill to be on the right side of things. We love sides. But our scope widens, and soon we have trigger fingers with sights aimed not at sin but at anyone who trespasses; we're longing to call the shots. Hate offers an equilibrium between hope and despair, until it consumes us and the gospel is forfeited when there's not enough grace for those kinds of people.

We went from church to church for a while without settling anywhere. My parents' eyes would scan a parking lot bumper to bumper with glossy cars while we chugged into the slot with our old Volkswagen van's engine coughing and moaning like a lawnmower. Heads turned and eyes stared.

They began to resent the church, although they never said so in as many words. Instead, Sunday morning's alarm was snoozed a few too many times and then eventually not set at all. On the mornings we did attend, there were always complaints. The message was too long-winded, the pastor used too many illustrations and not enough Scripture. Or enough Scripture but was dry and boring. No one greeted us after the service; instead we stood around by ourselves, or they made everyone awkwardly turn around and greet each other, making stunted attempts at small talk. The youth group wasn't big enough or small enough or they didn't have one. There was always a reason not to go back.

North American faith nearly killed us. It teaches that faith is really a well-executed plan to be followed only if all the pros and cons have been calculated and the backup plan is in place. North American faith teaches us to sit back and let the professional Christians do the heavy lifting. That faith and calling is in better hands if you're a white male with a seminary degree. It teaches us that patriotism is akin to holiness and the Constitution holds equal place with the Bible. It teaches us we are blessed to be a blessing, but all we see is hoarding and tiny kingdoms built around successful careers, four-bedroom-three-and-one-half-bath homes with walk-in closets and good schools, and an appalling disregard for anyone who hasn't managed to achieve those goals on their own. So often the church says all is grace but frowns on those who actually need it.

North American faith taught us it is possible to please God without any faith at all.

Instead of buying into the American dream of health, wealth, and safety, my parents clung to the idea of church as an ethereal global body we were part of in theory but which cost us nothing personally. We pledged solidarity to Jesus and his martyrs and missionaries both past and present but no one you could talk to about marriage problems or financial issues. No one you could grab a cup of coffee with or pray with. No one who would bring you soup if you got sick or watch your kids if you needed a date night. No one you would disagree with and have to love anyway. No one who would say the wrong things or offend you. We said we don't need to attend a church, we are the church, but we belonged to a bodiless, faceless one where no one could hurt us anymore. We belonged to a concept, an ideal, but no flesh and blood. Serving God had cost everything and we had nothing left to give.

But as imperfect as the churches were, we weren't any better off without one. Our bitterness festered within us. We sat in judgment of so-called Christians and their narcissistic gospel. We loved God, but we couldn't deal with his people. The church became a caricature of everything wrong with Western society, and we couldn't see past it.

It's no secret I've had decades of issues with church remaining long after I made my peace with God, and I know I'm not the only one. So many people have been devastated by churches they've attended. Some truly horrific and appalling abuse, corruption, and violence has been perpetrated and justified under the banner of church authority or Scripture. Some of you barely escaped still clutching to the fragments of your faith; some walked away altogether. Sometimes the gospel is perverted to lay a heavy burden on those who most need mercy and grace, who most need a Jesus who meets them in their pain. And I promise you Jesus is that and so much more. For you readers, I want to offer grace for where you are.

While I believe wholeheartedly in the words I write here and I indeed might not be around to tell this story at all if this wasn't a chapter in it, I understand that for some, it might be painting with too broad a brush. There is a marked difference between an abusive church situation you should run from and one that is healthy even if deeply flawed. I am writing about the latter. If you've been abused, if your wounds haven't yet turned to scars and you feel raw even at the mention of church, please know God is not okay with what was done in his name and justice will come. We can take comfort when pursued by the Good Shepherd who leaves the entire flock for one lost sheep, we are hounded by a God who comes for us no matter how far we wander. We are met with an unrelenting mercy. May God gather you under her wings like a mother hen, a shelter and a refuge under her breast.

But there are also many who, like me, are just fed up and frustrated. We have a justifiable list of grievances and scars we carry from the church. We want out because we're tired. We want out because we're disillusioned and the church doesn't meet our needs anymore or it never really did. We never stop to think maybe part of being a body is that we show up not only for ourselves but to help meet the needs of others.

Who Is My Neighbor?

The day after the 2016 election, friends called and messaged asking me how I was doing. I was grieving. There's no outcome that I could have rejoiced at that year, but the lament from friends who were hurting and scared was more than I could bear. The cry of the church, howling with the pain of anger and misunderstanding, accusations and defenses, pride and grief, was too sad to behold, and in it all, those same struggles were bound up in my nerves.

I watched friends and family choose sides and plant themselves against each other. I saw it mirrored in my tendency to want to do the same. To be justified, instead of seeking justice. To want to be merciful to some but not to others. To choose grace, but only for those I think deserve it. Oh, the hypocrisy in me. We become more concerned with our stance than with our surrender. How easy it is to stand against one thing only to find you're becoming what you're against.

It's easy to pride myself on loving the heart of God and want to see that reflected in the church.

I care about justice—give me the poor, the weak, the outcast, or the other, and I become mercy to their wounds. I care about grace—give me the lost, the broken, the weeping wanderers, and the misunderstood, and I will sit with them. I will weep with them and feel every tear. I will offer space to come and meet my Jesus.

Maybe it's because I know I am all of these things. I know what it feels like to have a broken mind that won't obey me no matter how hard I pray, or have faith, or cry out to Jesus. I know what it feels like for answered prayer to be a kind psychiatrist and antipsychotic meds that work. I know what it feels like to have a sick body, to lie in hospital beds, exposed and vulnerable and hurting, and to know that being seen and understood goes a long way toward killing the pain. I know what it feels like to be other, to be called racist slurs, to be judged by the slant of my eyes or the contours of my face, by the amount of space I take up in this world. I know what it is to speak and not be heard, to speak and be misunderstood, to speak and be hated. I know what it is to be used and discarded. I know what it is to always come up short, to wonder if there will ever be enough. I know what it is to be so lost, you can't even remember where you started.

I also know what it is to be ransomed and loved back to life.

When I think of my neighbors, I think of the least of these and my heart is overwhelmed with tenderness. But lately, I've realized when God asks me who my neighbors are, they have never been those the church classifies on the other side of the cross. That comes easy for me.

What is hard is not the man robbed on the side of the road, beaten and left for dead. I have felt those wounds in my very soul. What is hard is loving the priest and the Levite who crossed to the other side of the road and passed him by, presumably on their way to do their holy work.

When Jesus asks me who my neighbors are, the hardest answer for me will be the church people I most disagree with—the ones who spout hate, the ones who endorse it willingly, those who discard the *imago Dei* in the people I love, the ones who can't enter into another's pain. It will be the ones immersed in Christian culture who brandish Scripture like a weapon against the lost instead of an invitation to come and see the kingdom of God. The hardest answers are the ones I've judged, the ones I think don't deserve grace because they're the ones who don't seem to offer it to others.

"But wanting to justify himself, he asked Jesus, 'And who is my neighbor?'" (Luke 10:29 HCSB).

When Jesus asks me, "Who did I command you to love?" I know exactly who he's talking about. Maybe you do too? Maybe they're different for you. Maybe for you it's those liberal-left protesters in Black Lives Matter T-shirts blocking traffic on your way home, or those right-wing Trump supporters chanting "Lock her up!" at one of his rallies. Maybe you can't imagine you're called to love that transgender teen or that refugee you think is a threat to your very safety. Maybe you can't imagine you're called to love the ones calling for a Muslim ban or yelling "Build the wall!" but we are. We must contend against the lies that tell us the image of God is not present in those "others."

We talk of love. But to love, to be loved, is to be known and valued as intrinsically worthy of belonging. To love and to be loved is to be a neighbor, to be a friend, to be a body. We have made grace contingent on a list of right thoughts, right actions, and conditions. Grace is not grace when we charge our neighbor a great debt to earn it.

We think it noble to stand by our convictions, when really we're standing on them, building our own platforms of righteousness and justification. We use them as an excuse to draw lines in the sand, but Jesus bent low to the earth long ago to scribble in the dust before an offensive woman. Someone who would have been decidedly uninvited to the table. Jesus set the outrageous standard of belonging. He didn't condemn her. He offered her life. Do we forget that we are that woman?

We have itchy pharisaical fingers that want to palm stones to throw.

A Scandalous Kingdom

We must not call evil good, we don't have to turn a blind eye to injustice, we don't have to accept everything someone does, we don't have to go along with the status quo in our churches, but we do need to commit to love above all else. If the root of our actions isn't love, it's nothing but spiritual excrement. If our standard of belonging isn't who Christ died for, it's a sham.

We all have our own appropriated guest lists, and we will be shocked and appalled by who is embossed on God's. It's the one whose invitation to the table would make us squirm, pull at Jesus's sleeve and whisper, "Don't you know what kind of person that is?" And Jesus does, he knows exactly what kind of person that is, because he suffered and died, a man wrapped in eternity, God come down to bleed into the wounds we inflict on ourselves. We're going to have scars too if we want to look like Jesus.

How can we love the gospel and believe in its power if we honestly think anything we do or don't do—whether goodness or sin—determines the kind of grace that reconciles us to God? Only Jesus, only Jesus's blood and death and resurrection will ever amount to any accounting for my everlasting soul. It's the most preposterous kind of grace, the kind we can't earn or negate.

If we believe ourselves too repented or too godly to sit at the table with sinners of the worst kind, we somehow believe ourselves too good, too deserving, too lovely to know the wretchedness of our sins that forfeited life and chose death at every turn but for the grace of God. If human goodness is the pinnacle, then wild and costly grace is a scam. The biggest one of our times. But if offensive grace is the truth, it is the hope in the darkness, the salve for the wounded, the answer to all the questions, and the love song of our Savior. We will be seated with Jesus at a table set before both murderers and martyrs, and while all of us want to justify our space there, being poor in spirit admits we come like beggars hungry for grace. We enter with nothing accounting for our presence but the blood of Jesus.

If this grace is true, a weary world rejoices because we have been claimed by a devastating love. But sometimes I'd rather have an effortless love. I want an affinity group, not a community, not a body, not a church—only a Savior for myself, not a King of a vast and scandalous kingdom. My husband's cousin Pete, who is a pastor, says, "It's not community until someone you don't like shows up." Truer words were never spoken.

Christian community proves difficult for me. I've come to love the church, both local and global, but that often makes things harder. When church was nothing more than a Sunday to-do—a place to go sing a few songs, listen to some sermons I've heard a million times, and skim over superficial conversations—it didn't affect me because I wasn't connected enough for it to matter. It didn't cost me anything but a little extra sleep on Sunday mornings. These days, it's my idealism that stunts me. The same idealism my parents carried all those lonely years in Albuquerque. I don't want to love anyone enough to be disappointed. I don't want to be disappointed or hurt and have to choose to love anyway.

Give me the guts of Jesus's church and I'll want to look away. I'll want to stay home. I'll wish that God had some other less messy method of demonstrating the kingdom of God besides his people. I'll wish I had a different answer when Jesus asks me, "Who is your neighbor?"

But loving the heart of God will always call you toward uncomfortable love; there isn't any other kind.

Breaking Bitterness

When I was a teen, my parents were called back to uncomfortable love, and it saved my life. The breaking down of bitterness and resentment against the North American church didn't come from finding their kind of people, the ones who understood all of their views and held them in the same way.

It came from entering back into poverty, into weakness, into dependence on the very body that had first wounded us so deeply.

The crushing of bitter fruit began with a plea for help and the subsequent response from a wholly imperfect church.

My parents had been invited to meet up in Colorado with some old missionary friends and leaders they'd known in Holland and Nepal during those early days, when my parents' hearts were more zealous than weary, more fruitful than bitter. Years in Albuquerque had taken their toll, and reuniting with people who "got" them was too tempting to refuse.

But on their return journey, my parents found themselves stranded hundreds of miles away when their car broke down.

Financially incapable of affording the repairs, they had no choice but to ask for help.

Their need was apparent, they had no options to fake it or pretend they were self-sufficient; they were trapped. Since my brother was eighteen at the time, he'd convinced my parents he was responsible enough to stay home unattended while I stayed at a friend's house. They reached out to the mother of one of my brother's friends to let her know the situation since Jordan and I were still at home. She contacted her church, and even though they didn't know my parents, they helped them get the car running so they could get home to us.

It was then that they started attending church again.

This church saw a need and they met it. They didn't ask my parents to prove their worthiness to be helped. They simply loved my parents in the most practical way they could, asking nothing in return. And my parents' hearts softened.

I could tell you this church met all of their needs, the worship was heartfelt and meaningful, the preaching was powerful and theologically excellent, the congregation was unified and glorifying God in all they did, but that wouldn't be the truth. This church was flawed. As flawed as any church, the congregation made up of the same old sinners, the kind just as likely to hurt you as heal you. But my parents realized God was calling them to repent and commit. That for them to return to church wasn't so much about Sunday service or checking off a legalistic attendance box. It was about faithfulness, forgiveness, and letting go of bitterness in obedience to Christ who loves and died for his church, even with all of its flaws. How can we be new creatures with the heart and mind of Christ and still choose to hate what God loves? God showed my parents that interdependence was at the heart of God's vision for us. Even when we've been let down before. Even when it's hard. Even when it costs us.

Suffering Servant

So often we talk about how Christ knows our deepest pain and walks with us in our darkest moments, in our weakest times, in our most unbearable suffering. I couldn't trust a God who didn't understand that infinite ache. It's all true, he is the God who embodies our pain and incarnationally took on all of our sin and agony, even unto death on a cross. But sometimes I think we forget about our sharing in his suffering. How we are called to righteousness not retaliation in the face of persecution. How he asks us to pick up our cross and follow him, to find our identity in him and persevere with the fruit of the Spirit.

We rip up the roots of bitter fruit when we grow in love, joy, peace, patience, kindness, goodness, faithfulness, gentleness, and self-control. This fruit grows only in relationship. What good is patience with no offenders of our tolerance? What does kindness prosper anyone with no recipient of our tenderness? Who are we faithful to if there is no object of our faithfulness? When we speak of perfect love, we know it "bears all things, believes all things, hopes all things, endures all things" (1 Cor. 13:7). And God is perfect love to us. The fruit of the Spirit flow out of relationship with God, but they operate in community. We were never to remain insular and separate from each other. We belong to each other, but that is a high price to pay when it means dying to ourselves, our agendas, and our judgments, and loving our neighbor as Christ loves us. We are not just a part of a body for our own good, we are part of a body for the good of the whole. But we're so used to asking, What's in it for us?

When we identify with Christ's suffering, we count the cost. We realize we will be uncomfortable more than we'll be comfortable. We'll be displaced more than we'll be settled. We will be offended, we will be frustrated, we will be misunderstood. Yet still, we are called to rejoice when we share Christ's suffering because we are promised glory revealed. So many of us are unwilling to gather in this pain because it's always vulnerable, it's always awkward, it's always costly. When we are hurting, so many of us end with, "Take this cup from me," and never get to the part where we say, "Yet not my will, but yours be done," and mean it. We don't "rejoice insofar as you share Christ's sufferings, that you may also rejoice and be glad when his glory is revealed" (1 Pet. 4:13).

We reflect the holiness and sacrificial love of God in a miraculous way when we choose to identify with Christ's suffering, not just when he identifies with ours, and what the world desperately needs is a church that looks more like Christ and less like a parody of how to be respectable, comfortable, and safe.

It's much harder to let bitterness go, to forgive rather than fester in our own pain, but Jesus came to plant new seeds for the harvest. You'll find yourself hard-pressed to love Jesus well and not find yourself affronted by his incessant demands that we love like him. And he was always right there making the separate belong.

Maybe instead of our trying to flash our golden ticket, church will be more like a banquet table where we all come banged up, ragged, penniless, and starving to the feast set before us. Where we continually make space by expanding the table and the guest list doesn't offend us so much as make us gasp in awe at the magnificent grace of a good, good God while we sit elbow to elbow with our enemy.

six

I Walk with a Limp

The Hope of Brokenness

We are beggars here together. Grace will surprise us both.

GORDON W. LATHROP

My parents attended church in Albuquerque for a while, and during that time, my older brother came to saving faith, but I was the last holdout. My parents gave me space and didn't force me to go to church with them, but I knew they prayed that I would come to know Christ. My dad would say, "I believe God has a call on your life, Alia," to which I would roll my eyes and mumble something like, "Yeah right, that's never going to happen." I wanted nothing to do with God.

They got another ministry job offer in the middle of my junior year. It would mean packing up our family, selling our house, and moving back to Hawaii.

They sought the Lord while I pleaded with them to turn it down. I had created an identity for myself, I had a boyfriend and a life, and I didn't want to follow their stupid god to some island to do "mission work." I knew how that had turned out for us in the past.

In the midst of their praying, they both felt strongly that I would need to consent to going before they felt a peace about it. Unbeknownst to me, they were waiting for me to accept it and agree to go. I didn't know this the day my friend and I ditched school and instead drank 40s while sunbathing on rocks in Elena Gallegos Park all afternoon. I didn't know this when I came home less than sober and heartily agreed to move to Hawaii.

It made no difference that later I retracted my consent and sobbed angrily and rebelled in every possible way, including but not limited to ditching school and getting busted for flipping and totaling my friend's car while driving without a license. Until then, I had always been the good girl with exceptional grades and wholesome friends—on the outside. I called home and checked in, telling my parents where I was even if it was all lies. I always made curfew. I was a skilled and proficient actress and my fabrications were flawless. I was so good at pretending.

My brother was the one who punched holes in the wall, got into fights, or got expelled from school. He was the one busted for shoplifting and flunked out. He was the one who tried to hang himself on our back porch when I was in middle school, the one who took up most of my parents' emotional energy. He was the one they were always worried about. I gave them no cause for concern, I was the well-adjusted one who always seemed to do just fine on my own.

We didn't talk about things like mental illness. We didn't go to the doctor or the dentist unless something was really wrong. We were not good with maintenance, or indeed self-care; we were always just trying to survive. It's no wonder I wasn't diagnosed with bipolar disorder until I was in my thirties, even though I started showing signs of it in my early teens. I was just trying to survive too.

We went to mandatory family counseling after my brother's attempted death by suicide, but the assigned therapist spent most of her energy blaming my parents and trying to get us to confess they were horrible or somehow negligent or abusive. Only they weren't. They were human, broken, fallible, and doing the best they could with what they had available to them. So my parents focused on keeping our family together, while taking all the blame for everything that had gone sideways.

But as they began to heal, to find that language of hope that had been silenced for so many years, they began to feel that old familiar ache in their hearts to serve God in unconventional ways. They never fit in with nine-to-five, punch a clock, pay the mortgage, and save for retirement normalcy. They wanted more than ordinary. They still had some idealism lurking in them. Once they started pursuing going back into full-time ministry, all options meant moving.

When it was decided we were packing up and starting over in some far-off place, I had no reason to pretend anymore. They were dismantling my life. The tidy facade I had created for them to allow their peace of mind and my freedom was of no use to me anymore. To them, my unraveling just solidified their decision to move. Little did we know that if Albuquerque had been the desert, Hawaii was the wilderness.

Great Expectations

When we arrived in Pahoa, my dad surveyed the house the ministry had provided for us. It was unlivable. I don't mean it wasn't to our taste or the carpet was an ugly color. I mean it had no interior walls, only a concrete slab pooling with puddles of mosquito-infested standing water, no plumbing, and heavy green mold scaling the crumbling cement ruins. The jungle loomed in around the house, unruly vines strangling the walls and breaking through shattered windowpanes. No one had flown to the Big Island to inspect the house or property for years, and it had become uninhabitable, squatters gutting it over time. We lived in Nepal in the early '80s in a dung-style hut, so we'd never be accused of being high maintenance, but this was ridiculous.

The ministry had also provided a vehicle, which amounted to an old Mustang that looked more like a Pinto. Its exhaust fumes leaked into the car; we had to drive with the windows down so we didn't asphyxiate. This would have been bad enough, but it also rained for forty-two days straight when we first arrived. We had to sit in the passenger seat holding a towel up against the window, droplets running down our arms and soaking our clothes anytime we left the house.

The rain in Pahoa fell in constant sheets, pounding on our metal roof like an assault being sieged against me. And I took it as that. A personal attack. I sat on our back porch, which consisted of a slab of concrete with a tin covering, listening to the rain pinging like rapid gunfire while dragging hard on my cigarette until the cherry blazed with all the fury I felt inside. This was my personal hell.

And I mocked their God openly. If I had thought God was ironfisted and mean, a secondhand god of scarcity before, now I just thought he was plain vindictive. This is what your God provides? This is the way he rewards obedience? My foolish parents had offered their lives again and again in service to this stingy deity, and here we were right back where we started—homeless, with a broken-down car in the middle of nowhere. *Nice.*

Before we ever moved to Hawaii, I had all the fuel I needed to hate God. I practiced for years. It started with church but it spread to hating all of Christianity and eventually to God himself. How could a good God have such jacked-up people who claim him? How could a loving God allow so much pain and suffering? How could a merciful God allow the trials I had seen firsthand in my family? How could God let me suffer in the ways I had? I found no answer to satisfy. And now this?

Your God is laughable, cruel, and impotent, I cried.

My parents knew we couldn't live there and contacted the ministry that had hired my dad. They agreed to pay half of the rent for a small rental after seeing the conditions of the "home." At the same time, my father got another job offer to work for the Salvation Army, which included an ample salary and livable accommodations. Again, they fasted and prayed. Maybe this was God offering another path? It was certainly more secure, and so far, they had every reason to feel betrayed by the ministry they'd uprooted and moved their entire family for.

I knew nothing of this at the time. But my mom felt strongly they should remain obedient to what they believed God called them to even though things were bleak. My mom, who budgets everything and will travel to three different stores to save a few bucks on toilet paper or chicken thighs, who reuses all of our old sour cream and yogurt containers and will wash and rinse Ziploc bags, who's cautious and tentative with everything, threw caution to the wind and did the most absurd thing. She said to wait on the Lord. Wait and see.

My parents felt quitting would solidify my view that God wasn't trustworthy. He does not provide for his children because he won't or he can't. And so they dug into the small amount they had gotten when we sold our home and rented a sparse house with catchment water, a slab of concrete in back, and a tin roof to overlook the unyielding downpour. And like God preparing Noah for the floodwaters that would bring new beginnings, it made little sense.

When the Flood Comes

We still had no furniture and couldn't afford to get any now that we had to pay rent. We had two lawn chairs in the living room and a futon pad on the ground.

I remember hitchhiking for the first time as a teen not because I was rebellious or wanted to take rides from strangers but because our family car had broken down and there was no other way for us to get home. Again.

Reconciling my years with a loving and merciful God seemed impossible. I could not believe in a God who continually abandoned us. I hurt everywhere. I fit nowhere. Home wasn't a place I could feel. And I met God there. Or God met me. In our home that wasn't a home.

It rained those forty-two days straight, and I considered taking my own life right there on the chipped and cracking bathroom linoleum. But I didn't want to break my mom's heart. I had seen the devastation a suicide attempt can leave. I had seen it in her eyes years ago when her gaze nervously traced the raised red scar that had turned into a grotesque palette of purples, yellows, and browns on my brother's neck. She'd meet his gaze and see the whites of his eyes clouded with blood where all the capillaries had burst from lack of oxygen. I couldn't forget that haunted look she carried whenever she looked at him.

But I was as sober as I'd ever been, and it was its own reckoning. I had no transportation, no license, and no hopes of getting one anytime soon with the impending charges for my car crash. I was miles away from any sort of civilization and it was still raining! Our house was its own haphazard rehab. Only now, the torment I had propped up and pushed away came crashing in and I had nothing to hold it back.

My brain abuzz with thoughts, wild and tangled, I felt frenzied and agitated and in so much anguish I just wanted to make it stop. In Albuquerque I had learned all the ways to silence the torment. I was the girl who ran too loud to keep from having to sit with the questions. I turned up the volume and lived a blaring existence. I didn't know I had bipolar disorder. I just knew there were times my skin tingled with restlessness, my limbs possessed, my feet tapping out a Morse code. I felt invincible, immortal, immune to hunger and thirst and the incessant demands to slow down, to sleep, to recharge. My mind was a colony of secrets, schemes, and shenanigans. I palmed the key to the mysteries and the world unlocked before me, right before it unhinged completely and came crashing in on me. It's an unfortunate law of the universe: what goes up must come down.

I'd roll the car window down all the way and let it blow my hair wild like the mania I felt inside. My fist thumped against the dashboard humming with the baselines of my mixtape while my friends passed the bottle that burned the length of my throat. I rode along the windy mountain roads, each switchback pushing me against the cold door frame while I tried to keep the embers of my cigarette from burning holes in my clothes. I flicked the ash into the endless black I couldn't escape no matter how hard I pushed on the gas.

Drugs made me feel like a god for a moment, and that scared me a little, because there might really be a god and what then? Would I go to hell if I overdosed? Would I go to hell no matter what?

As a child, I lost myself in imagination and story and seemed to all the world a perfectly happy girl. And maybe I am remembering more into my past than existed. It's easy to look back with the insight of thirty-five years and see that little girl, delicate and frail, as she fingers the pages of her favorite book, the one that's illustrated but not on every page. It's easy to imagine she understood her pain. She knew everything hurt a bit more than it is supposed to at six or seven. But how would a child know how much life is supposed to hurt? How would a child know that for all her days, she had accumulated more than her share? And what is an appropriate share of pain?

I've lumbered through a lifetime of it and only recently pressed into it instead of pulling away.

As a teen, I'd gazed wobbly-eyed and knock-kneed into the empty bottle, fingering the sides for another pill. To make you numb. To make you beautiful. To make you see or unsee. To make you whole.

I wondered if I was born with too many nerve endings. If my very soul was run through and coursing with every fiber needed to pick up and receive pain like a network of cables transmitting nothing but static. The fuzzy nothings of a life with no clear images. If in fact I was bundled so tight with synapses, packed end to end and top to bottom, that the very entrance into this brutal world devastated me from the word go. And every bruise from then on just deepened the bloom of sorrow. One can only manage that kind of pain for so long before nerve endings surrender and shut down, fraying and sparking like old wire, ready to burn everything down.

When the heart is damaged beyond what one can endure, the body begins to shuttle blood away and cordons off the broken bits. This shock often kills trauma patients before blood loss or the injury itself.

I lived all those years in this emotional state. Thready-pulsed and dizzy, lungs screaming to breathe. Wandering icy-eyed as my gaze skimmed over the world around me. Heart unable to pump and fingers numb. And the only quiet came when the pain was pushed down far enough, numbed by a deep-fingered plunge into pills or boys, food or things.

But I cannot escape my sobriety. I am trapped on a slab of concrete, seemingly adrift in our ridiculous box of a house in the middle of a jungle with forty-two days of unrelenting downpour.

I cannot love with a heart this broken. I cannot feel anything but the dismal beat reminding me it is not yet over. And I long for it to stop even as I rise and breathe and walk around in skin that never seems to cover me right.

And I face the rain and remember my childhood. I remember the voices coming for me. I remember following and hanging back and hoping to be invisible. I remember the monstrous shadow following me, and I hope no one else can see it. But it's there, crouching at my heels; it's everywhere I go. The devourer of beautiful days, the one who taught me the language of despair and doubt, of shame and silence.

And then the world is nothing but a terrible and infinite dark.

Until I'm blind with tears, ransacking the medicine cabinet and rifling through drawers. Coming up empty. Until I decide it's time to quiet that thready hum once and for all. Until I decide it doesn't matter if my mother will always be haunted by my ghost, or if the preachers who spit and pound the pulpit are right and I will burn in hell for this.

I cannot imagine any of that right now because my mind is a fathomless inferno, the scorch of the world blistering every inch of me. I only want the shadows to disappear and the voices to stop and I believe with all of my broken heart this is the only way. I am blown glass, combustible, I will shatter into a million pieces across the universe, I will return to dust, I'm just searching for the right sledgehammer to collide with. And I'm so scared my hand shakes as I pick up the flimsy disposable razor because I don't want it to hurt. I don't even know if it will work. I remember to cut from wrist to elbow, tracing the path of my bloodlines. I remember all the days I offered my veins in hospital rooms as a child while my parents prayed for a cure. But there is no cure for this life, no solace. How often I've felt myself punctured and drained. *The whole world is a bloodletting and not one of us is being healed.*

I don't want to make a mess my mother will have to clean up, and I wonder if this is a cry for help or the real thing as

I hold the razor over my skin trying to build up the courage to make the deep cut.

I've flirted with death before, but just enough to blow my hair back, just enough to make me feel the tiniest bit alive. But I've never gone all the way. I know you can't come back from that. And my mind ricochets through it all, pinging and clanging against the edges, ripping through all rational thought, just like the rain that never stops pelting the tin roof with unholy clatter. And I cry, no, scream out to God, that I never asked to be born! I never asked for any of this! And I never in my wildest dreams or crazed-minded fantasies imagine for one second that God would answer me. But he does.

And I find myself silenced, barefoot and open palmed, splayed like an offering across the floor, and the monstrous shadow voice that stalked me since I was a tiny thing lies dashed by glorious light. And my heart kicks back into rhythm. The resuscitation of grace. I breathe again.

Making Sense of Miracles

After that night when I was ready to take my own life, and instead found myself laid out by God—physically knocked to the floor and flooded with a peace I, to this day, cannot fully describe—I began to make excuses.

One moment I was at the end of myself, cursing at God and in so much pain, I had worked myself past all the anchors tethering me to this world. The next I felt the presence of God from the place on the floor where I'd landed. And it was like nothing I'd ever felt. Like hope, like peace, like mercy. Maybe this was grace? Maybe God isn't distant and absent. Maybe God reveals himself to desperate girls on chipped linoleum floors in the middle of a monsoon and says, "You belong to me. I have loved you with an everlasting love. You are mine." But that was all too much for me to fathom.

I am not now nor have I ever been what I would consider a woo-woo Christian. While I absolutely believe the Spirit still moves and works miracles, I remain critical of some of the more charismatic claims I've witnessed. I've seen too many faith healers and prosperity gurus peddling heretical promises guaranteeing the will of God can be manipulated or bought for the low price of this seed offering made out to the name of their ministry. I've had preachers pray for me to be slain in the spirit while pushing their oil-drizzled thumbs firmly into my forehead, willing me to go down while people around me flopped on the ground like dying fish and laughed, babbling like maniacs.

I've known people attempting to cast demons out of their car when the engine wouldn't start only to admit they forgot to get gas on the way home and their tank was empty.

I've seen faith and deliverance weaponized and used against the hurting. I've been told the only reason I still have bipolar disorder is because I don't have enough faith to be healed. But I believe God can heal me. I also believe he is under no obligation to obey my will. Still, at that time, I wanted something to explain away the very real and terrible possibility that God existed and that he wanted something from me.

I thought perhaps it was my body's response to all the stress hormones and cortisol levels and my legs just gave out. Maybe it was some sort of evolutionary self-preservation system and my body just collapsed as a protective mechanism? Maybe I had some sort of mini-stroke? Maybe it really was shock?

But even with all my own justifications to apply reason and logic, I could not deny that I felt something I had never felt before. I felt God. My parents had given me a Bible I never used and instead wedged under a tiny garage-sale table in my room to make the legs even. I pulled it out and began to read it at night behind my locked door. I didn't want my parents to know. I didn't want my dad to say, "I knew God had a call on your life, Alia Joy." I didn't want any spiritual I-told-you-so. I started in the book of Job. So began my long night wrestlings with God.

Wrestling with God in the Dark

My bed was a rolled-out length of eggshell foam, the kind you put on a mattress should you actually have a mattress, a whisper of softness not thick enough to keep my hips from falling asleep and aching through the night. As I read my Bible, I was confronted with the questions and fears that were ever present. I'd lie in the dark with God and whisper prayers into the void, hoping someone or something was there answering me back.

Like Jacob wrestling with God through the night, this grappling changed my identity and renamed me. Like Jacob, who had tried to manipulate and manage blessings by deception and self-protection, I too became the great pretender. When God initiated this match, Jacob was consumed with anxiety that Esau was coming and would slaughter him for his deceit. God could have just showed up and told Jacob everything was going to be fine. But when God initiates our wrestling, it is not because he is cruel. It is not because he is withholding his blessings or comfort or unwilling to provide for or protect us.

In the wrestling, in the questions, in holding on to God and not letting go in the darkest night when we cannot even see his face, when anxiety floods our soul and we have lived a life of so many lies, we just might find ourselves transformed. We might feel the touch of God dislocating our hip as dawn breaks. God might take us to the ground. In that tremendous pain we might cry out in desperation, "I will not let go unless you bless me," and there, with our throbbing bones, God renames us and says you "shall no longer be called Jacob [the deceiver], but Israel, for you have striven with God and with men, and have prevailed" (Gen. 32:26, 28).

It's interesting that when Jacob first prays for protection and deliverance from Esau, he prays to the God of his father Abraham and his father Isaac. Yet after he has wrestled with God and his prayers regarding Esau were answered, Jacob erects an altar with his new name, Israel. He names it *El-Elohe-Israel*, which means "God, the God of Israel."

When we wrestle with God, our faith is etched on our bones. It erases death and offers new life. It becomes personal. We name our altars to remember. There is no secondhand God and there is no secondhand faith. God is no scarce deity; he is not holding out on us. Instead, he brings us to that place of weakness where we are disjointed and he strengthens our fragile and imperfect faith.

This weakness doesn't leave us more vulnerable before our enemies, real or imagined. Instead, it trusts that even though we walk with unsteady feet, we can rely not only on the God of our fathers, but on the God who reveals himself directly to us. A God unmasked, a God who lets us grab hold of him in the darkness. The weakness that remains testifies that God is infinitely merciful and loving and that his greatest good is always for our flourishing even if we are initiated into the great abundance only through our profound lack.

I haven't arrived unscathed to this place. I carry the bruises of those restless nights, of a too-thin mat and a paralysis so severe I could only be laid at the feet of Jesus. Somewhere along the pages of my life, I lost faith that God was good. It took debilitating weakness to see his goodness.

Sometimes I remember that whisper-thin foam of my youth and the ache in my hips and the limp in my step as I wrestled with God. I think of my parents choosing to stay, to wait on the Lord. I thank God for their obedience. For helping bear witness to the goodness of God in that horrible rental where I first believed.

These days I have an ankle injury that flares up from time to time. I broke it in my twenties, only I never went to the doctor because we didn't have insurance, and what I thought was a bad sprain at the time healed wrong. I never know what's going to set it off, but when it happens, it's excruciating and I can't put weight on it. Sometimes, I still find myself limping, and when I do, I remember what is formed in the brokenness, in the weakness, in the ache. I came back to life in that home that wasn't a home. The place I'd meet my God; the place I'd learn I'd always been called; the place I'd meet my future husband, who would become home to me.

To this day, when I can't bear the weight, Josh drapes my arm over his shoulders and I lean into him and he holds strong as he carries me home.

It was always the plan that in the midst of the catastrophic brokenness in this world, grace would surprise us all.

seven

Where Home Is

The Hope of Ordinary

The ordinary arts we practice every day at
home are of more importance to the soul
than their simplicity might suggest.

THOMAS MOORE

A few months after I came to know Jesus, the ministry my
parents committed to, to wait and see, had my dad visit a
piece of land on the other side of the island to inquire about
possibly using it for a rehabilitation center. It was currently
being used by Youth With A Mission in Kona, but only one
family lived on the farm at the time. They were on staff and
worked with Deaf ministry. My dad returned after touring
the farm and meeting with the family.

"They have kids about your age," he told my brother
and me.

Great, I thought, still hesitant about church and Christians—especially the kids of some random ministry family my dad wanted to set me up with. They were probably pious weirdos who spoke in King James English, wore denim jumpers, and would certainly judge my nose ring, Doc Martens, and Beastie Boys T-shirt.

It wouldn't be the last time the one whose judgment was off was me.

His name was Josh. He was a year older than me, seventeen to my sixteen. He was kind and adventurous and uncomplicated. Even though he wasn't my type and I was still pining for my ex-boyfriend in Albuquerque, I needed a friend. He did too. My brother, Jordan, and I started hanging out with Josh and his little sister, Anna.

Josh grew up in a Christian family also, but in his teens, he'd slipped easily into the hedonistic draw Hawaii's shores offer. He was a good-looking surfer with no limit to partying, girls, and drugs. A few weeks before meeting us, he'd felt the emptiness of endless parties, getting high, and meaningless sex. But everyone he knew, his entire peer group and everyone he surfed with, partied. To be different was to be alone. He prayed, "Lord, I want to know you. I need some new friends. I need to stop living like this."

A couple months prior to that prayer, Josh, ever the adrenaline junkie, paddled out into a hurricane swell and the waves pulled him farther and farther out. His arms burned from paddling and the boy who never worried about anything so trivial as mortal danger was terrified he wouldn't ever make it back to the shore. He prayed one of those bargaining prayers something along the lines of *if you get me out of this, I will do better*. We are so good at trying our hand with vows of surrender and Boy Scout behavior when we have no choices. Like my dad in the storm many years before him, he cried out to God. Still, like my father decades earlier, God heard him. Josh couldn't escape the Holy Spirit. He couldn't shake the conviction that there was more to life than smoking pakalolo and catching the perfect wave.

Jordan and I came into his life at the perfect time. We banded together, an unlikely group of new believers finding our way.

I had known Jesus for only a few months when I met Josh, and I had all the zeal of a new convert. I wanted to change the world—I never imagined that would start with me. I dreamed of untamed adventure and wilderness callings. I wanted to be the fiery voice proclaiming the path to an audacious faith. Even though I'd hated being a missionary kid growing up because of all it had cost us, when I became a Christian myself, I reverted to those ideals. I still resented the church and believed the best way to live out my faith was in another country. I idolized radical service and sacrifice as the only way to please God, and to me, service and sacrifice was denying myself and picking up my cross on a dusty road in an impoverished nation. I had no idea that the cross God would call me to carry was a life of ordinary faithfulness. That I would instead be tasked with recognizing the poverty in myself and bearing witness to the goodness of God in a life I never wanted.

I never dreamed of picket fences and dinners around the table with my darling offspring, making conversation about the high and low point of our days. I never wished for a husband and a mortgage and matching throw pillows for our tastefully decorated living room.

As a girl, I never rocked baby dolls and pretended I was their mama. My dandelion dreams sailed on turbulent winds with my hopes of escaping into the open. I always believed the wild girl who lived in me would be set free and I'd make my mark on this earth. I didn't know the mark I'd make was a grave where I'd bury dreams and what would grow in its place would look nothing like I'd ever imagined.

I dreamed of Africa and huts and red dirt that stained my toes and planes that whisked me off to my great calling. I wanted to live out a risky faith, untethered and transforming the world. I despised pew sitting and antiquated Americana Christianity. I saw it as a relic for all the lukewarm, the average, the ordinary. The ones who took the message of "GO make disciples" lightly. The ones who refused to budge at all, who would rather stay and build their tiny kingdoms of affluence and comfort. I was, after all, my parents' child. For me, faithful was overseas missions.

I thought a call meant to do something for God, so I determined I would live fully the call of God on my life. But I never imagined that the call for the last twenty years would be to stay and walk faithfully with God while struggling with mental illness, unable to be involved in any "ministry." I didn't know my ministry would be words often written from hospital beds or in recovery. That I'd shake out my story with trembling hands and I'd testify to a God who meets me here when I haven't a single thing to offer.

These days, I struggle with the word *calling* in Christian circles because it tends to make some people very certain and others wring their hands and wonder what the heck they're supposed to be doing. *Calling* feels like a cruel joke when you're hurting or suffering, when you're weary or poor or ill, when you're confused or struggling in your faith, when you're weak and it sounds like another to-do that you can't manage. So I prefer to think of calling as telling the truth about God, bearing witness to the world in all of the ways unique to us and our story.

It's being honest and vulnerable and open to the work of God in small and tender spaces. It's revealing to the world the image and character of God in the ways specific to how he's created you. Everyone will do it differently, but no one can do it like you can. There are no unnecessary parts in the body of Christ.

We get tripped up when we start trying to tell other people's truth instead of our own. Trying to live out a calling we think is bigger or better or more important than ours. I'll be honest, I wouldn't mind a different story. My health limits my capacity. I am reminded that on my own, I am finite, dependent, powerless. This is my ministry of weakness. It's easy to resent our own limitations and to look around and think everyone else got a bigger slice of the pie, a bigger payoff, a better purpose than bearing witness to God's goodness in the middle of a life of lack. But when we sow envy, we reap fear and discontent. When we sow grace, we reap peace and acceptance and mercy. Not just for ourselves but for others. We flourish under the truth that we were specifically created for the kingdom of God.

My calling looks like answering my children's thousandth question on days I'd rather zone out or escape to my room for some quiet. It looks like making lunches for my husband to take to work and making amends when marriage feels like the hardest calling of all. It's faithfully loving a church that doesn't meet all my needs, line up with all of my theological foibles, or have a community of people I instantly click with because we have everything in common. Instead, I'm called there to see the beauty in being stretched.

I've spent a huge part of my Christian walk waiting for the Great Calling. The thing I wanted to do, maybe even the thing I felt I was made for, instead of embracing the place God had established me in.

I've spent too many years frustrated with the *now*, yearning for the *after*. But every day we make choices that end up being our eternity. The after is a result of what we do this very moment.

Every day we walk in obedience or we don't. Middle ground is a deception. It's not so much about the details we get bogged down in as it is about the heart to seek love, to flesh out faithfulness, to pursue holiness right here and now without waiting for the right ministry opportunity to show off our skills. We fool ourselves when we think we have to sort out all the specifics and line up all of our dreams before we obediently surrender to the call of God on our lives. To live beloved. To love our neighbor. To abide in Christ. To keep fluent in hope.

> Jesus said, "Love the Lord your God with all your passion and prayer and intelligence." This is the most important, the first on any list. But there is a second to set alongside it: "Love others as well as you love yourself." (Matt. 22:37–39 MSG)

In all honesty, this mothering gig can be hard. Marriage is beautiful and tough. Loving others often tests every ounce of my patience. Writing has been both a gift and a trial. Ordinary life has been the hardest calling I've ever answered, the hardest thing to bear witness to, because who could possibly care about the mundane and ordinary life? I had no idea the depths of my own selfishness until asked to share myself with my family. To lay my will down day after day and seek God's. To write in relative obscurity and tell the truth even when no one was reading.

It isn't the atlas pins and circumnavigating the globe; it isn't writing the book or speaking in front of crowds; it isn't anything tweetable or worthy of an Instagram filter. It isn't accolades or huge leaps of heroic faith that make up my calling. I can't put it on a résumé or impress you with my accomplishments.

It's the small things that go unnoticed. It is the moment by moment choices, the constant release of my will and my resting in Jesus, that form this life of faithfulness. It is the hard work of the everyday and the remembrance that God is at work in my unspectacular moments, of which there are many. It is remembering God's mercy when I can't seem to feel it at all. It is building altars of praise because I'll need the reminders that even still, God is good.

For me, calling doesn't look like mountains being moved or seas parted. Most days it looks like a seed buried, ever changing from day to day but unnoticeable to everyone above ground.

It is the secret place where faith breaches the husk and it feels like death and so much darkness. It feels risky because you can't see why this would matter. How could these small things mean anything in the kingdom of God? It feels like brokenness and abandonment. Like God created you with dreams and passions and intellect and yet they feel useless in your ordinary life.

~~It feels too small, too irrelevant to ever contain the call~~ ~~of God, but it's this attention to the ordinary stuff of earth~~ ~~that points to God's goodness.~~

Josh and I were just teenagers when we met and fell in love. We imagined we'd travel the world together. We even imagined we'd change it.

He bought my wedding ring for $99 and the small Taiwanese woman joked, "Chubby fingers, good sex life," and winked, offering her plump fist in a flourish of fingers. We smirked like the kids we were. No adult had talked to us about sex so candidly. And certainly not as it pertained to us having it. I didn't blush but felt like I was supposed to. Demure was the role a good Christian girl played. My prior years attending youth group and listening to sermons on the evils of fornication, promiscuity, and causing our brothers to stumble before marriage were in conflict with the absolute blessing of God and enjoyment we were supposed to have once we said "I do."

I didn't know how to flip that switch from bad to good. Still, I was wearing white, even though I'd been told often enough growing up in the church that I hadn't earned it.

I never got that promise ring all the other girls at church had. The promises I kept were of the darker variety. Closed doors and secrets. I wondered once, when I was a girl, if I slipped my friend's promise ring on my finger when I saw it lying on her dresser, would it singe my flesh like an omen? I didn't dare.

But I was wearing white for my wedding. I had my dress in a garment bag in the closet. I didn't love it, but it was what we could afford. It was good enough. I didn't think the wedding was the point. I had a practicality that contradicted my romanticism. I had big dreams, yes, but I also knew when something was fantastical, a fairy tale always out of reach. I knew how to settle.

I don't know that I believed in happy endings by the time I walked down the aisle. I believed in good enough. No matter how hard you try to shake him, the god of scarcity is a sticky deity. It's so easy to conflate contentedness with being resigned to a fate that is always only good enough. It's easy to feel proud that you aren't fussy, that you're not high maintenance, that you're grateful—when really it's more that you feel you don't deserve anything extravagant. You don't deserve abundance. You don't deserve the goodness of a kind Father. But the reality is that goodness, it's everywhere. It's in the ordinary moments we allow ourselves to see.

On our wedding day, I walked down the aisle to a CD playing Pachelbel's "Canon in D Major." We had no sound system. We literally had a boom box plugged in at the back of the chapel. The chapel was small, and the song is long, so when I got to the front of the aisle, our friend, who was in charge of the sound, hit Stop and the song skipped and halted mid-note.

I remember my hand trembled when Josh slipped the ring on my finger. It caught on my knuckle, and I thought of the woman at the jewelry store. Chubby fingers. We wrote our own vows. I made promises that day I had no earthly idea how to keep.

We kissed. It felt embarrassing in front of our parents and grandparents and friends. We'd never kissed in front of anyone, not in a church. Not so obviously in front of God and witnesses.

But he took my hand in his after, and he led me down that aisle as man and wife. He, with the biggest boyish grin, for that's what he was: a boy.

We didn't know how long to stay at the reception before we could leave. Before we could pull the bobby pins from my updo, a style I would never wear again, nor want to. Take off his tux.

Pop the champagne we were a couple years too young to legally drink. Get flesh to flesh.

Isn't this what it's all about when you're a good Christian couple? The ban is lifted and you can be, what? One? Naked? Not ashamed of all the stuff you tried so hard not to do all those years before he put a ring on it?

We're driving to the bed-and-breakfast. A gift from my parents. We stop at a gas station. I am in my wedding dress, he is in his tux.

We go in for snacks, for a pack of clove cigarettes and some chips and salsa. We were too flustered to eat much at the reception and we are ravenous. And maybe, this hunger, this approved hunger, this normal hunger, will staunch the awkwardness between us. The car is silent when we climb back in. We stare straight ahead. But it's heavy, the anticipation, the reality, the weight of what we've just done. We're man and wife. But aren't we just kids?

I reach down and rip open the bag of tortilla chips, grab the salsa jar and twist. Maybe in eating first, we will once again be a boy and a girl who are about to live a whole life together doing things as mundane as changing the oil and setting the alarm for work, picking up the kids and prescriptions and groceries, watching TV in bed together.

I dip the tortilla chip in the salsa jar, but I can only get the corner in and I have no container to pour it into. It needs to be poured out to be more fully tasted. But I offer it to Josh anyway, cup my hand under so it doesn't spill, and lean over to his mouth. He keeps his eyes on the windy mountain road, whiplashed across the Hawaiian jungle, and takes it from my fingers. My chubby fingers.

I think to myself, *Maybe this is the beginning.* Letting ourselves be hungry in the most natural ways. Letting ourselves be fed. And when it's time, letting ourselves be poured out again and again in serving each other. Maybe this ordinary life isn't a secondhand one, a consolation prize for those who didn't get the promise ring or the innocent childhood or the dream wedding.

Maybe our ordinary is not just good enough. Maybe it's good.

Part 3

Strength

eight

Let Us Rejoice and Be Sad

The Strength of Lament

We must learn to regard people less in the
light of what they do or omit to do, and
more in the light of what they suffer.

DIETRICH BONHOEFFER

Before I considered myself a Christian, my life was littered
with lost things. I'd raised angry fists at God and wondered
how Christians could speak of his loving-kindness when all
around me I saw devastation. But after I became a Christian,
I automatically withheld my weak and broken places from
God. I began to instinctively tidy myself up. Fix yourself for
Jesus was never the good news, but so many of us default to
this. Sure, brokenness made sense for non-Christians; they
didn't have the hope I did. But after I became a Christian,

I slipped into a relationship with the same reliable and safe God who offered no solace for my parents. The God who can be managed with more prayer, and more faith, and more Bible study and Scripture memorization. A God I didn't have to fear. A God I could understand but not know. But in order for any of that to make sense, I had to believe that the only thing that mattered was eternity. Some far-off hope where things would be made right, but no answers for the moments in between. No hope to remain in the middle space where many of us live our days—our whisper of "Lord, I believe, help my unbelief," dangling from our trembling lips. I'd been taught doubt was the sin that would undo me and send me back to the darkness before God. I came to believe faith was never entertaining doubt and its demonic mothers, sorrow and suffering—the dragging underbelly that birthed doubt. I never entertained that eternal question: Is God good? Faith meant silencing the questions, sentencing them to the furthest corners of my mind where I'd keep guard against them.

I didn't know then that sorrow is sacramental. Sorrow is sacred. Suffering is not an indictment against God; it can be the single space we identify most deeply with Christ, who knows it best.

I had been a Christian for years; I knew the lingo. *Everything happens for a reason. God works all things for good.* Instead of a dark underbelly, there was a silver lining. I faulted myself for not seeing past the storm clouds; I wasn't trying hard enough to choose joy. So often church teaches us to hide our true selves, to cover up our anguish, our rage, our brokenhearted longing for a better story.

Believers claim verses about hope and joy and standing firm in our faith. We flip to Romans 8:28 and slap it onto every painful occasion, every trial, every sorrow. We want to skip ahead to the good things, instead of coming as empty and battered as we truly are, offering nothing, and believing that Jesus will see us every time. We're uncomfortable to stand before a crowd of witnesses and fall at Jesus's feet while everyone sidesteps our desperation and judges its inappropriateness. Being poor, or broken, or needy is something we fight against. We have taught a tidy life of carefully chosen roads and avoidable obstacles. But the reality of following Christ is that there is nothing tidy about it.

Christians lie when we sell a packaged and sanitary way of following God. We offer a discounted gospel when we say it will fix your problems, ease out the wrinkles of your day, give you shiny, full-bodied hair and perfectly behaved children. We wield our Christianity like an omen to ward off hard times. We want a warning sign or someone to blame when things get broken. When children die. When dreams fail. When we are summoned to great and immeasurable loss and the hits keep coming.

A Devastating Grief

I awoke hours before the alarm clock went off. I curled on my side and placed a hand on my swollen belly, hollowed and echoing a raging emptiness.

I showered that morning, letting the hot water run down my face, mingling with tears. My eyes were puffy, the whites traversed with spidery red lines. My ragged, wet hair dripped onto my bare shoulders like I was being pulled down and drowned by the weight of my pain.

147

The week before, we sat, anticipating another heartbeat. But the thud was missing when my doctor rubbed warm jelly onto the ultrasound wand and waved it over my belly. Like a magician saying *abracadabra*, the screen came to life, a whoosh of static and a faint, immovable outline. His hand slowed. He furrowed his brow then and called me "kiddo" as he explained how things had gone so wrong. How there should be movement and a fetal heartbeat, how the silhouette of my baby was not a magic trick, it was a disappearing act. An apparition, a loss, how the flutters I felt were never going to get stronger.

We drove to the hospital in silence. There weren't any words worth saying.

The doctor explained everything again while Josh rubbed my hand, churning it in his as if wearing smooth a prayer bead.

I signed papers and undressed. I put on a hospital gown and removed my wedding ring, handing it to Josh. He helped me climb awkwardly into the bed with the railings locking into place like a trap. And I laid my arms open, offering my veins for the start of an IV. I counted the tiles in the ceiling as they wheeled me under the fluorescent lights, clearing my mind out by filling it with nothing.

There was a rush of people in and out, a swish of hospital scrubs and stethoscopes and the ragged rip of the blood pressure cuff. The thud of my heart pumped in my ears.

It astonished me that my heart could just keep pumping when it had already broken.

I was asked the same questions over and over as the shifts changed and my bed was wheeled into pre-op and post-op. They asked me to state my name and birthday and what I was being treated for as they checked my chart and lifted my arm to match it to my paper wristband.

My voice was even, a monotone recitation. I was there for a D&C. A little over sixteen weeks. Alia, and twenty-two years old. And then I would add miscarriage just in case. So they would know the baby they were taking from me was already gone. My body had failed me again.

I awoke groggy, my throat sore and raspy, my IV tubing falling across my face as I wiped at my eyes, waking to a new reality. And later, when I was discharged, I pulled on my stretchy pants, belly still swollen but hollow all the same, and shuffled out of the hospital.

Saying All the Right God Things

I wouldn't ask questions like *why* out loud. When Josh and I lost our baby, I thought faith was saying God works all things for good and leaving it at that. Well-meaning people told me God needed another angel. They told me God has a purpose for everything. They told me other people had it worse, at least I had a healthy kid. They told me I was young and could try again.

I'd seen others live a life devoted to their grief. But I feared that conceding to the pain and asking hard questions belied a small faith, not enough trust in the sovereignty of God, and too much focus on the here and now. I believed eternity was what mattered, and getting there had less to do with flourishing here than it did a blind devotion and total white-flag surrender to whatever came my way.

Secretly, I worried God might not have the answers to my questions, so I summed up life in Bible verses, in parables and tidy lessons, hoping to absolve God for the suffering and loss I felt. I wanted a shortcut to bypass the pain. I wasn't sure my God could stand up to the scrutiny if I let loose all my doubts.

So I learned to fear the unknowns, the emptiness, the messiness of life and indeed death. I feared faith. I wanted certainty and promises I could control. I wanted a God I could contain within the highlighted portions of my study Bible, not one who met me in operating rooms filled with death.

But grief pushed down comes out sideways. It's taken me years to learn to adequately grieve lost things.

I wish I had known that sometimes this life will ache with emptiness and it's okay not to rush to fill it. It's okay to leave some questions on the books. It's okay to be angry and to admit we can't see the good of it all right now. To sit on the floor in my baby's room and weep over the blankets and the onesies and the car seat that would be packed back up.

It's okay to grieve the lost things you held only as the flutters of hopes and dreams. It's still loss. How else do we make peace with the present?

I wish someone had told me it was okay to relent to sadness, to doubt, to the divine ache and the catastrophe that is death. We can lie on a gurney with God and allow the sorrow and suffering its due. We let God reckon with death, and we acknowledge that things are not as they should be and we are not the only ones offended by the tragedy coming for us all. I wish someone had told me it was okay to succumb to anger, to the great and formidable *why*? I wish I had understood that God is undaunted by my humanity.

I wish I had understood that answers are not the reason we ask the questions. Sometimes we ask the questions to say,

Who are you really, God? Who are you to me right now in this pain? Where are you now? Are you here with me now? Can I trust you're not relegated to some distant eternity, sitting on a silver-lined cloud, but instead in this sterile and silent room? The questions are the place to admit our need, not just for answers, but for awareness of who God is.

I wish I had known the questions are the invitation for Jesus to enter our sorrow and reclaim the dead space.

I wish I had known Jesus is the God of all lost things.

We live in a world of fractured dignity. We rise each morning to the lament of a sin-scarred existence. We see it in the headlines, in the cracks and fissures and gaping wounds of the church, and if we're honest, in the mirror as we gaze in wide-eyed horror at how easily our hearts wander and break. And sometimes every solution is a Band-Aid on a hemorrhaging wound, because our solutions often try to sidestep the reality that this world hurts. This world is filled to the brim with lost things. We've all had death etched on our bones.

Surprised by Suffering

So often, we're surprised by injury and inconvenience, by suffering and circumstances. We've reduced our gospel down to a formulaic set of rules whereby the faithful sidestep the pitfalls of this fallen world and instead float unscathed and isolated through their good life. We want it all and forget there is always a cost. As C. S. Lewis so eloquently implies, we want safe instead of good.

If we fail to dig into a theology of suffering and the way we as Christ followers will hurt right alongside a troubled world, we write off people's trials as an anomaly or a reaping they had coming instead of a place we connect with God's solace and peace and even our purpose in walking with and weeping with those who weep.

We love to make excuses and write off pain as a lack of faith and offer remedies and platitudes and never push in deeper to community to help carry a burden stretched wide and intended for the whole church to bear.

We are a culture with no room for awkward tears and pain that can't be fixed. We hide our shame when we are not enough, when we are weak, when we are anxious and burdened, when we don't have the answers. What does the gospel offer us in this pain if we cannot be people who grieve even as we believe? Where is the God who resides in cancer wards, war zones, grave sites, and gutters?

Let us pour out the oil of gladness and praise from our lips but let us not forget the wails and cries and pounding fists. God is here too.

You Can't Talk to God Like That

I remember reading the book of Ruth as a new Christian, and I came to the verse where Naomi says, "The LORD's hand has turned against me" (1:13 NIV). I thought, *You can't talk to God like that.* It seemed blasphemous somehow. Shouldn't she have been a stronger believer who trusted God even in the face of such loss? Especially since her daughter-in-law was watching her relationship with God. Isn't Naomi being a bad witness? Wouldn't it have been a more powerful story if she was widowed and lost both of her sons and was a destitute foreigner, but she told Ruth not to worry because

God was faithful and would provide for them? Wouldn't the steadfast thing have been to tell Ruth that God is good and they had nothing to worry about?

I didn't understand it then, but years later, when I had endured a different measure of grief, loss, and suffering, I saw something different. I saw a woman who didn't stop praying even when her words were bitter. I saw a woman who still calls God Yahweh, admitting that he is constant, the great "I Am." Naomi remains in covenant with Yahweh and travels back to Bethlehem. She acts in faith even though her heart is broken and frustrated. She is achingly honest about her emptiness and need. God wanted her lament to bind her to him.

The Ministry of Burden Bearing

So often we've been trained to have all the right answers and be ready with a verse, or a quote, or an uplifting anecdote that we forget that sometimes the ministry of burden bearing goes further than advice we toss out from a distance and instead means some heavy lifting.

Are we people who bear one another's burdens well? Or do we spend most of our time trying to convince them that it couldn't possibly be that heavy or that they don't have that much further to carry it?

Sometimes I wonder if all our pep talks are really more to insulate ourselves from the reality that sometimes we have no answers for suffering. We are like Job's meddlesome friends, inaccurately pointing our fingers this way and that, trying to pin it on someone. We trust that nothing is lost that is surrendered to him because he is a God of constant redemption, but that doesn't make those ashen places or empty wombs any less awful.

Could we be people who confess our great and unending need to one another and be met with Jesus? Could we be a church where doubt and dependence are welcome to be explored together?

If we believed that God can and does call us to a life reliant solely on him, would we not also believe he calls us to a life relying on each other? I often think of Jesus's life, and how he chose dependence for himself. He chose to rely on a young unwed mother to protect and defend him, to later wake with his swaddled infant body and put him to her breast all hours of the day and night. He trusted his sustenance would come through the nourishment of another. He relied on his disciples and the generosity of sinners to help meet his physical needs. His entire life on earth, Jesus chose to insert himself into humanity and risk being denied, risk being betrayed, risk being misunderstood, risk being lonely, risk being judged and ridiculed and eventually killed. Jesus took on flesh, and we have this vague concept what that means. But for him to model this dependence, this fleshly weakness, for God to have scars means the world got close enough to leave its marks. It means he was vulnerable and open and dependent enough to fully invest in people even when he knew the outcome would cost him. As the body of Christ, are we not one flesh who mourns and rejoices as one? Why are we so bad at belonging to each other?

We like to talk about how God works all things for good, especially when it's not our circumstances that are a mess. Don't get me wrong, these things are all true, as God's Word says, but it's just human nature to want to shine things up when someone close to us is expressing doubt, or loss, or grief. It doesn't mean we have bad intentions or that we're hurtful people—sometimes we honestly think we're helping.

But as someone who has been on the receiving end of a lot of "let go and let God" and "sometimes God shuts a door and opens a window" pep talks, it can feel reductive. Especially if that's all we're ever hearing from God's people.

We are taught to tamp down any arguments and to consider outrage, anger, and doubt crude and unnecessary for kingdom work. Truth becomes a pinnable quote or a pretty printable, but it doesn't have a way to deal with the horror of grief or the absolute shock of suffering. It has no answers for evil, racism, violence, injustice, or oppression. It cannot sustain confrontation and is lulled by inside voices and the need for everyone not only to get along but to agree. It cannot sustain doubt. It has no answer for the marginalized, the poor, or the pitiable. Injustice is something God will fix later but we don't get our hands messy now.

Learning to Lament

What if instead we were a people who learned to lament? What if we believed faith was less about blind devotion to all the right answers and more of an invitation to come fully into relationship with Christ and be met in our most desperate and confusing moments? Lament isn't some patch slapped onto hard times to make them more palatable but an admission of our profound weakness and inability to carry a single thing on our own.

Lament isn't simply about feeling pain. It is a cry of injustice; it is the piercing howl of protest against evil; it is confession and petition, and even praise. It screams that death has wronged us, but it will not have the final say. When we ask God why he has forsaken us, it is the language of intimacy that trusts our agony will be heard and answered. If my suffering has taught me anything, it is just how bold I can be with God in my distress.

God does not expect us to remain stoic when our hearts are rent. We are not asked to put our masks back on so we don't embarrass God with our suffering. We are not better Christians when we call the hardest parts of life "good." But we can learn to call God good in the hardest parts of our lives. Admittedly, understanding love was easier before grief touched me. It remained buoyant, intact, simple. Floating on lofty ideas about loving thy neighbor or thine enemy. The *after* cost more. Love overtook me with weight and fullness, impregnated with possibility, I dare say hope, but bleeding from its palms.

Jesus Isn't Afraid of Our Humanity

Jesus paid attention. Jesus wept. Jesus broke bread and laughed with his friends and healed the sick. He tucked himself away to rest and pray. He went to parties and took naps. He walked this earth in a body that could easily be broken. He said come unto me. And in so doing, he royally ticked off a lot of people who despised how common he made grace. But Jesus knew how to read the room. When we look at Scripture, we see Jesus offered comfort, presence, and mercy, but he also met people's needs right where they were. He fed them and healed them and served them. He gave them water, washed their feet, and helped them fish. Jesus didn't fear the fleshiness of our existence, our frailty or our failings. He came near, God with us. As Christ followers, we must be willing to practice the art of nearness. Of with-ness. There are a myriad of human emotions that are difficult to sit with, to engage, to carry. During a tender and wearying time, it's often easier to promise someone the happy ending than to accompany them on each agonizing step in their long walk of obedience.

Lament says you belong to me, and I belong to you and will enter in with you. It is Ruth linking arms with Naomi and vowing, "Your God will be my God and we'll make the journey home together."

Jesus knew what it was to endure someone's anguish. He knew what it was to see people, to lock eyes on our desperation, to not turn from our sorrow, our despair, or our weakness. He was never offended by our humanity; he chose it for himself when he walked among us.

So often when we are hurting in church, we put our masks back on and pretend everything is fine because we think our testimony is supposed to be our faithfulness. But our testimony is only ever how God is faithful to us, not the other way around. When we try to keep up the pretense for too long, we grow further away from God. To stay in relationship with God, when our worlds turn upside down and nothing makes sense, he invites us to lament. How amazing that a sovereign God is not offended by our big feelings. How amazing that he comes near.

How Long, O Lord?

When we are bewildered by our distant, unseeable God, we don't turn away; we live into the tension that even though we are afflicted and feeling forsaken, our gracious and merciful God is still our God. It dismembers our doubt, because we can honestly express it. Like the psalmist, we can cry out, "How long, O LORD? Will you forget me forever? How long will you hide your face from me? How long must I take counsel in my soul and have sorrow in my heart all the day? How long shall my enemy be exalted over me?" (Ps. 13:1–2).

These days bipolar disorder and physical illness have claimed so much. I mourn the lost things, my life soiled by invisible sackcloth and ashes. I tear at my clothes, collapse into a heap, and allow my heart to wail unrestrained by the confines of social norms and polite company. I am a madwoman, beating at my breast, lamenting the suffering of a mind so broken it feels like a thousand stinging pests let loose in my hair.

I tell God I cannot endure this. I ask him to take this cup. I beg for mercy. I confess I need help to believe once again. I carry these things clumsily, my mind falters so easily and some days all I have on my lips are the Psalms to ask, *Why God?* Just the questions and the assurance that he knows even when I don't. Just the prayers of a million needs and aches and the swirl of tragedy that dusts our ashen world.

But sometimes in the midst of those prayers, I feel a glimpse of kingdom glory and the kind of love that makes no sense and the kind of brave that inhabits the hearts of humanity when God is in us. I feel a tenacious grip of hope wrestling its way through the despair, and what comes out is praise. That native tongue swelling with the language of God's people. Hope. Can you imagine this? This praise. In the face of the absurd and horrific and terrifying. Because after lament, I am always found again in him. All who belong to him will never be lost. I know this as surely as I know anything.

The Language of Lament

In lament, we find language that boldly comes before God and trusts him to show his face. To cover us and guide us and ransom us. To fight our enemies and restore the barren places. In lament, we acknowledge we are powerless to fix it. The good news is God never asked us to. We cry out from blood-soaked asphalt and hospital beds, from grave sites and war zones where artillery shells have punctured so much more than the rubble at our feet. We cry out over empty cribs and jail cells, from protest lines and church pews. We cry out after biopsy results and making the side of a bed that will never be slept in again.

Lament is subversive, always lifting from the breasts of the suffering; it's always born in pain. Our tongues swollen with agony. It is the untamed cry of our hearts. The truth of our witness.

We are not called to housebreak this truth or make it more palatable by neutering it and making it play nice and behave. The truth will not sit and fetch and stay, it demands to be unleashed. It is wild and dangerous. So often we've made an idol of image and the status quo. Sometimes the church is so busy scurrying around trying to protect our testimonies that we've failed to bear witness to a broken world because the truth is too ferocious.

Sometimes I sit in the dark with a silent God, in the death of dreams, and the disaster of middle spaces, and I say, this tenderness, this holy ache, this wailing sorrow? This is not our great liability. This is our gift, the costliest one we'll ever carry. Unwrapped, it's opening to another's pain. Offering in return our burdened broken hearts as a reservoir for corporate lament. It demands divine strength. Eternity keeps account. No tear is lost. We carry them together.

How then do we speak truth to power, breaking down wrong things, while building bridges to connect us? How do we become truth tellers living into our purpose? How do we have honest conversations with God and about God?

The peacekeepers live in an opaque world where no truth can penetrate. They're so insulated, they don't recognize their own great isolation. They've stockpiled a bill of goods for the long haul and taken care of their own. They say, "Peace, peace," where there is no peace. They've built great walls to protect themselves. They say unity when they mean uniformity. They say "settle down" and "anger is a sin." They say "fix your eyes on eternity" as they blindly watch the borders grow taller. They numb their weakness, they deny grace, because, "Haven't we done just fine for ourselves? Aren't we #blessed in this great kingdom we've built?" They dismiss the faint sound of wails and protest beyond the great walls they've built around their safety and comfort.

The cynics live in a transparent world where they shine a glaring light on and call out everything and it is garish and harsh, exposed and raw. They are crusaders, ransacking houses, so busy dragging everyone into the street to be tried and stoned. They'd summon hellfire from the heavens if they could, to scorch the earth and all its inhabitants, without remembering they'd be eaten by the flames too. They scream and point fingers and accuse, composing vicious tweets dripping with their own enlightenment, but their hands are so full of stones to throw, they have no way to welcome anyone. They haven't learned how love covers a multitude of sins. Their devotion to destroying leaves everyone bare, cold, and naked.

But the people of God are called to be peacemakers. We see the beauty and the brokenness. We face the world sober. We aren't passive in the face of suffering, oppression, or injustice. We listen to the cries, we echo them in our hearts. We get our hands dirty, not with stones to throw at others, but with the rebuilding of the kingdom. We remember we are counted among those needing grace—we are the ones who would get scorched by the fire or drowned by the flood if not for the mercy of God. We have earned nothing. We know grace, because the light found us. We are translucent, shining the glory of God in a world gone dark, even in the dark places of our own lives. We have access to God. He hears our cries.

nine

Starving to the Feast

The Strength of Dependence

The most effective pulpits aren't sturdy
wood, they are broken people.

A. J. SWOBODA

A few years ago I spoke—no, I preached—and the message
was simple: when I am weak, he is strong. I said, "Weakness
is a holy invitation to allow grace to do its work." And I
asked, "What if weakness was a spiritual gift?" but what I
was really wondering was, *Is it mine?* Was my spiritual gift
"weakness," specifically? Could that even be a thing?

I'd felt the cost and knew the worth of weakness because
I felt the Spirit of God carry me through. I'd been limping
for so long.

I sat in my room at JumpingTandem: The Retreat, legs crisscrossed like a little girl. My friend Deidra Riggs had invited me to come share, and I was scheduled to speak about the Art of Truth Telling the next morning. I was getting ready for sleep when I had this nagging feeling God wanted me to tell a different story, a story from my most tender and raw places—not places I was looking back on fondly with tidy lessons learned, but places I was still struggling through. I stayed up half the night rewriting my entire session, knowing I wouldn't have time to go over it or practice it or polish it to a high shine, and I hoped it was indeed the Spirit of God and not delirium from the prior weeks of near-constant sickness, sleep deprivation, and lack of oxygen to my brain.

I put in my earbuds so I wouldn't wake my roommate, turned on worship music, and started to type. I couldn't help but stop to lift my hands like a fool right there in my bed with my laptop perched on my legs and tears that guaranteed to make me look like a hot mess in the morning flowing down my cheeks.

That night God ministered to my soul more than he might ever minister to the people coming to my session. That moment was just for me. God might disrupt my life, draw me to places of unrelenting weakness, pull from me my most vulnerable and tender parts, and then remind me that poverty of spirit is the birthplace of all grace.

Pain and weakness made me keen and acutely sharpened my senses until I began to see it everywhere. It called out to me and demanded to be heard in a world that can't recognize God's goodness through its scars. And maybe in this great equalizer, the place where we all feel a little tender and aching, we begin to see each other more clearly. We're all marked with ash.

I shared about my experience in the middle of the night in a Facebook update. I wanted to hold place and have a reminder. An altar to return to before I'd done my session, before I could be swayed by results or delivery or performance. Before there was any feedback good or bad. I wrote down how good my God was to me, how merciful and kind and abundantly present he was in those early morning hours. I shared about truth telling and how grace unmakes bitter fruit, but the truth that kept coming back to me that night was that my God is good, even in the weary and worn-out places. Maybe even especially there.

In the morning, I broke a vial of asthma medicine into my nebulizer and watched it wisp like the breath of God into my lungs while I prayed for wide-open spaces and the emptiness to be filled. The past few months had been almost comical in how many health crises I faced. Almost.

In the months prior to and immediately following this encounter with God, I would experience two tooth abscesses (one that almost went to my brain), oral surgery, two extractions, eleven courses of antibiotics, two C. diff infections, influenza, bronchitis, severe complications from asthma, a gazillion nebulizer treatments, two courses of prednisone, eight severe migraines, five immediate care visits, three days in the hospital, four CT scans, two X-rays, a kidney stone, two ER visits, three kidney procedures, and two surgeries. And, if a treacherous body bent on betraying me in every imaginable way wasn't enough, I also continued to struggle with bipolar disorder, anxiety, PTSD, and have horrible split ends, so #thestruggleisreal.

I thought I'd have to cancel my trip altogether, but even though I was on my second round of steroids and a bunch of other medicine at the time, I felt well enough to travel. I hadn't factored flying into Denver and the effects the altitude would have on my breathing. I also hadn't known how bad the pollen would be in Nebraska.

I went to the first session and I immediately had to leave because I couldn't catch my breath. I stood in the bathroom, coughing, bent over the sink, tears straining against my lids. I used my rescue inhaler and still I couldn't get my lungs to take breath.

I wondered if I'd even be able to do my session. What happens if I can't breathe? What happens if I start coughing in the middle and can't stop? What happens if I cough so hard, I gag and throw up in front of everyone? Don't ask me how I know that's a scenario to worry about, but I do. Did I come all this way only to be unable to speak? In my desperation, I prayed, *Lord, if you will, even the rocks will cry out. Give me breath to share your glory.*

I could hear my friend Dana leading everyone into the presence of God with her gift of worship. A chorus of voices sang, "It's your breath in our lungs, so we pour out our praise."[1] Even though I couldn't get out more than a few words at a time, I felt God swoop low and near and gather me. It was my anthem to believe. I took a deep breath.

I stood at the podium shaking, with tears brimming and threatening to burst free, and it wasn't because I was nervous, although I certainly was. It was because my bones couldn't contain the fire I felt, the fire from these trials, the heat and scorch of God's refining embrace. My ashes had purpose. I was unleashed.

Witnessing Creation

I once saw creation. I witnessed an old Chinese woman spill shards of sand, soft and pure as milled sugar, into a furnace pot she called the *crucible*. The heat would melt any impurities that might have gotten into the sand mixture, for without pure ingredients, glass is unstable and useless—maybe even dangerous from the possibility of it shattering or exploding.

Over two thousand degrees later she dipped her red-hot wand and pulled out a sparkling molten orb. She leaned her head low like she was bowing and brought her lips to the other end of the wand before breathing life into what was once a million broken and fevered parts. The glass obeyed her breath, bubbling and bulging and stretching invisible seams. When it was rounded on the end of her rod, she wielded it like a composer, her tiny frame rolling it this way and that to accompany a silent orchestra. And then she stopped and carried it back to the heat.

She told us that while glass is being blown it often cools to the point where it's unworkable and rigid before it can be fully shaped. Only this time she opened a small crevice that gaped hot-white with a blazing center like a fiery tomb. She told us this is called the *glory hole*. This is where the glass is heated again to make it pliable. To make it beautiful. And when she pulled it back out of the fire, her assistant held it while she brought in the heavy iron tools. Sharp-edged scissors and giant tweezers pinched and stabbed and slashed into it in ways that looked random and haphazard. It hung suspended and oozing, stretching like a child's taffy. But she had a vision I couldn't yet see. Only she heard the notes to her symphony.

It began to take shape in lean branches like arms, no wings. It began coming to life and it was beautiful. Then she placed it into another furnace to harden, this one set at a high temperature that would gradually cool over time, helping to reduce the chance of it shattering. Glass is an amorphous solid lacking any clearly defined shape, structure, form, or function until it has fully set. Only then will that random alignment of weak and frenzied molecules hold shape and be made strong, able to endure the stresses of the world.

I watched this magic, enchanted by her fiery wand. I was seventeen, and I had only just recently passed through the flames and met God. I had big dreams and long hair that escaped my ponytail and blew free in the trade winds. I breathed in the scent of plumeria and soot, but at the time I only focused on the end product, a beautiful crane in flight with wings stretched as wide as my hope. Still, when I went home to shower, the smell of burnt things lingered in my strands.

It's so easy to remember only the finished form. I forget that it starts with broken pieces. I forget that heat gathers sweat on the artist's brow and her face flushes as she plunges the already broken pieces into the flames again and again to make her creation stronger. To make it useful and beautiful. To make it sing. I forget that the master's tools pierce and bind and rip apart, her wiry biceps cording up as she creates.

I forget creation felt the breath of God in the sand, whispered on bones, blown through and expanding our hollow lungs with new life.

I forgot what it feels like to be created. I didn't know when my lungs burned as I stood at the podium preaching the truth of all I had endured that God was composing my freedom song, my arms finding their wings. We are truly free when we abandon ourselves to the clarifying grace of Jesus with not one thing added. But I'm not going to lie, sometimes those flames burn everything to the ground and we find ourselves amid the rubble and ash wondering what Jesus could possibly be doing.

I didn't know my dry and weary bones were kindling for a spirit ablaze with the weight of God's glory. I spoke the words God told me in the middle of the night, and they breathed life back into me. God held the chambers of my lungs open for the entire hour, and I spoke of the hard and necessary places where God meets us, where God knows us, where God claims us, and I knew then that nothing is lost that is surrendered to him. I just had the blessing of seeing it this time. But I knew before I had spoken a single word that morning that something had changed in me.

My deficiency was the strongest thing about me because God was fully present in my lack. I literally had to call on God just for the breath in my lungs and the words on my lips and the strength to stand. And yet we are promised, "He gives strength to the weary and increases the power of the weak." And then he says, "They will soar on wings like eagles; they will run and not grow weary, they will walk and not be faint" (Isa. 40:29, 31 NIV).

Always We Begin Again

That was the session I met my future editor. After my talk, she asked if I had ever considered writing a book. This book. I said yes, but I didn't feel ready. I felt the message stirring, and I was putting down words, but I didn't feel it was time and I was in no rush. I thanked her and took her card for someday.

I didn't know then that I'd barely make it home without my lungs seizing on the return journey. That I'd find myself in a minivan cruising down the highway with writer friends one minute and suddenly having to veer off into a gas station—which, by the grace of God, was the first we'd passed in hours—to hastily plug in my nebulizer next to the nacho machine because my rescue inhaler wasn't cutting it. I sat there with the vapor wafting into my lungs while I gasped and wheezed, and my friends weighed whether to call 911. And as the chambers of my lungs started to loosen and open, I remembered the feel of fire in my bones and breath in my lungs. I could've died there in some random gas station along a highway outside of Denver, but God had more in store for me. Had I known what, I might've lain down next to the racks of Doritos and Funyuns and Slim Jims and asked God to beam me up. No one signs up for this, no one wants a life of enduring. If we knew at the outset, we'd choose another route. But this is why our weakness works in our favor. We have no other way home, just straight down the highway, on the open road, hoping to be able to breathe again. And sometimes God gives us back our breath because we're not there yet.

I didn't know that days after I arrived home in Oregon, I would be back in the hospital being prepped for kidney surgery that would include months of other complications and issues. That indeed this was just the beginning. Always we begin again.[2]

I had tasted the goodness of God, felt the weight of glory, and it helped sustain me. It made the unendurable endurable. Pain is not without purpose. Weakness is not the goal, it is simply the inevitable state of our humanity. But the by-product of having God redeem our weakness instead of removing it is that we are made strong in Christ. There are no work-arounds, there are no shortcuts. Like Paul asking God to remove his thorn and being told God's grace is sufficient because his power is made perfect in weakness, we too inhabit spaces where we cry for God to take away the problem, the pain, the puncturing thorn in our side, but we don't realize that might also take away the providence of God to meet and sustain us.

I know I am called to a small and humble ministry of weakness. Really, we all are. I know empty and weary and broken, but more importantly, Jesus does.

What if we started to see weakness not only as something to endure but as our spiritual gift? What if we didn't fight it so hard? What if we stopped pretending? What if we allowed grace to meet us there and resurrect the broken things? What if we lived as though we actually believe God's strength is made perfect in our weakness?

We want God's perfect strength, but we don't want to live with our constant, gaping need.

Everything in me longs to put my hand to the plow and create glory for God until I'm utterly unable and my resources are bare. But God was never interested in my strength; he's most pleased with my surrender.

Glory is revealed most clearly in desperation, dependence, and discomfort. The very areas we are prone to numb, to pretty up, to run from or deny.

Weakness is my spiritual gift. In my complete and utter poverty, I give up my illusion of control and my weakness becomes my greatest offering of worship.

When lost and adrift, shipwrecked and abandoning dreams like a sailor bailing water from a leaky vessel, I found myself open to the possibility that I am a whole version of me even when I am broken or weak or sick. Even when I am poor in spirit. Even when I feel I'm drowning, even when Jesus seems to be fast asleep through the storm. Sometimes he calms the seas, but sometimes he lets our ship of treasures go down—every shiny jewel and golden idol we thought had worth plummeting to the sea floor. Sometimes our lifeline doesn't show up until we're being shipwrecked. He meets us in the storm. I believe in the goodness of God not because life gets easier or tidier, but because in the midst of weakness I am carried by sustaining grace.

But I didn't always believe that. It takes practice.

A Lifeline

I first stood in line at the Walmart pharmacy to pick up my tiny orange bottle of pills that were prescribed like a lifeline, a desperate measure I didn't want to believe I needed. After the tears crashed down, and my doctor reached out and took my hand in his and called me kiddo, I couldn't shake the sadness.

But the sadness made sense then. We had lost our baby. I was unwell. Who could blame me for my despair? And when it didn't relent, he scribbled a prescription out on his pad, ripped it off, and handed it to me.

I sat in the parking lot as I fingered the side of the bottle and slipped a tiny white pill up and onto my open palm, placing it on my tongue and gulping it down like bitter wine. I tore at the label, scratching at the sticker with my thumbnail. I didn't want anyone to know I was taking an antidepressant.

I was embarrassed I wasn't enough. I was embarrassed I couldn't fix myself with more faith and more prayer and more hours dragged off the clock and spent in quiet seeking. I was embarrassed on God's behalf. He had made me wrong.

So I searched for sin in the wreckage, a sign that if only I repented hard enough for my lack, the darkness would rise and lift and his presence would fill the empty places where nerves and neurons had long since stopped being receptive and the deep pull of sadness had taken its place. But no amount of repenting for my weakness, for my inability to hold all the pieces of me together and be a good Christian girl who chose joy and fought off the darkness with some well-memorized Scripture, worked. The anguish inside me grew, but I couldn't surrender to my weakness for fear that this somehow disqualified me from being used and loved by God.

To Hunger and Thirst

I've barely survived depression at times. There are nights so dark they wolf down my days—all fangs and bared teeth under a moon thick as a lemon wedge bobbing in a sky full of sweet tea. But all I taste is the bitter. And even still, I thirst.

My tongue was long trained by Sunday school etiquette and polite society never to cough up unpalatable words like *depression* or *suicide* or *antidepressant* in church company. Instead, "fine" becomes my answer, so I choke down the un-savory words for fear of being the guest who fumbles with the finery and dribbles wine down the front of my shirt. Afraid

I would forget my manners in the house of God and rip into the bread with white-knuckled fists like it was life and gulp down the wine like my tongue was on fire.

We've become practiced at nibbling tiny, easily digestible bites and taking the daintiest of sips, patting at our lips with crisp white linen, but we all come famished to grace. There is no other way to be filled.

We are all beggars here, some of us just clean up better.

This is holy work. Living in desperate spaces, gathering manna and mystery in the desert.

It is always only enough for today. God keeps me hungry, but I'm learning each day brings nourishment. Those pangs, that soul hunger is meant to point us to the cross. To communion. To the fellowship of suffering. To the gift of resurrection and new life.

It's as though Jesus knew in the breaking of the bread and the pouring of the wine how ravenous we'd be in this world. And of course he knew. He knew exactly how much we'd need reminding that the brokenness of bodies and the blood spilt have purpose, because some days that's all we feel.

I longed for Jesus in the wreckage. My need for a Savior was as tangible as my stomach's groaning and pleading for food day after day, reminding me I am not autonomous from this world. I am not a stereotype or a label, a ghost girl or an apparition. I am embodied.

We are bound by our physical needs. But we are also bound by the needs of our body, and our body is always more than joint and sinew, marrow and muscle. Our body is a hungry church.

If you want to know someone's story, ask them about their favorite food. Food always tells a story. It is a language unto itself. Ask what their mamas used to make them when their noses were stuffy and they were coming down with something. And if there was no mother to bring soup or hot tea, well that tells its own story of hunger, doesn't it? Ask what they ate to celebrate. Ask what they would have for their last meal. Ask what they would serve you if you came over for dinner. Ask what was the first thing they learned to cook. Ask how they gather and where. Ask why even when you're full, sometimes you can still feel so empty. Because we all hunger for something.

We were created to be nourished. Fed. Sated. And yet, we are born hungry. We are born dependent and empty, open-mouthed and rooting for our place at our mother's breast. Even Jesus chose these humble beginnings.

Our bodies are sustained by the table. After all, the Son of Man came eating and drinking. On his last night, he didn't preach a sermon, he poured wine and broke bread. He said, "Eat of me." And when he rose again, his hunger followed; he went to the table and ate breakfast with his friends. Even his resurrected body teaches us about how we commune and celebrate and see each other.

But I had no energy to scavenge for sustenance. I needed Jesus to come for me. I needed manna from the heavens.

Live with Wonder

That holy hollow, that treacherous ache now allowed space to be interrupted by grace. The days slowed and became monotonous, a managing of sorrow and symptoms. On the days when my body waged war in every cell, I asked Jesus to show himself faithful and present.

I found him in beauty and wonder. An imagining and hoping in glory. A prophetic mindfulness. The awe of a God so big and majestic, we cannot comprehend it but we contemplate it all the same.

We can almost hear the Master's symphony. The music so thick we can nearly taste it. The violin swooning in a sultry soprano dripping notes from the strings like drops of honey. The sweet psalm pounding in our bones and rising like a fever. The melody reminding us we're always being created and will dance to a new song.

I lay in bed one night, the curtains wide open like a theater stage hosting an ensemble of stars. The inky-black midnight was thick with them, like tiny seeds of hope embedded into soil as rich and thick as coffee grounds, and I imagined the way that light navigated wise men across foreign lands seeking a King. The hope for us all.

I am a complete version of me, because no willpower or positive thinking or bootstrap mentality will ever complete what grace has already done. And this is the good news I so often missed during those years when holy wonder seemed a notch above me and continually out of reach.

The space illness has made in my life is painful but cherished. It slowed my soul enough to see beauty in peonies blooming by my bedside even though my nightstand was also covered with prescription bottles.

While I was stuck in traffic on my way to the doctor's office after months of physical illnesses and surgeries, I marveled at how the blushing sunset melted into the clouds like a swirl of rouge swept across porcelain cheekbones.

A wonder-filled life is grateful attentiveness to the awe in our ordinary.

I confess I am undone by the strum of messy chords on a battered guitar, by a perfect red lipstick, by children's laughter on the first warm day of spring, by the musty splendor of a dusty old book.

I am gobsmacked by the first bite of a ripe summer peach. I am moved by the sway of limbs and swish of hips when that special song comes on, by the old copper roof caught in the tendrils of tender sunlight, the architecture, and the brick walls embraced by creeping vine on the slow walk home. I am touched by everyday kindness—the casserole bringers, the lady in line who smiles in solidarity and lets me go first when my kid is shrieking. The ones who say, "You can sit here" and scooch over to make room. The ones who text, *How are you doing? I'm thinking of you.*

We are loved by the people and places and things we love. We are loved by the way we take notice when our souls feel alive, and the way we are reminded to live with wonder when our souls don't. To make contact with the world, to bear witness to the glory of our everyday ordinary. I unwrap my arms and gather my children, and on days when I couldn't get out of bed, they came to me and offered their tiny hugs, homemade art, and clumsy prayers. And it was glorious too.

They see the poverty in me, the deep, abiding hunger of a poor soul, the desperation for God, and they know it's not just about some Bible verses and making good life choices; it's not about having it together or doing more for God. They know there is a holiness I long for but it's born in the surrender, in the ever-expanding "Not my will but yours." It's born on the ordinary days, when I wonder, *Am I strong enough to live the life I've been given?* and God's answer to me, when I write down the reminders, is, *I am with you always.*

Pain breathed into me God's presence both as Savior and as one who is incarnate, taking on the anguish of this world to bring healing and redemption.

A God who breaks into the brokenness is the only One who could ever understand how desperately I need him.

So on the nights when I fold myself fetal on my couch and my body curls like a question mark, when I find myself famished, when the devourer gobbles up all the light and spits out endless midnight, I remember that honesty is our invitation.

There are so many among us who hurt, and we may never know we're sitting next to someone barely holding all the pieces together when we gather on a Sunday to sing rickety hymns and hear God's Word cracked open for us.

I can tell this truth because I've learned the ministry of honest words, of weak spaces, of holy dependence and admitting our deep hunger. This is not a litany of complaints, this is a lament of love. And sometimes, when honesty is our invitation, we find that those silent ones, the ones among us we never even knew were hurting, the hungry ones who can no longer hear their Savior's psalm, they come and knock at our door. We pull out a chair and welcome them to the feast.

Ten

The God of the Lost

The Strength of Being Found

I will take with me the emptiness of my hands.
What you do not have you find everywhere.

W. S. MERWIN

The answering machine clicks on after the fourth ring. I un-tuck my feet from beneath me and rise from the couch. I'm pacing back and forth, my bare feet on the cool hardwood floor. The ground is steady; it is me that is shaking.

I realize I am holding my breath waiting for a voice on the other end. I am nervous anticipation. I feel the bubbling in my stomach like the fizz of a shaken soda. I take a deep breath so my words won't come out rushed and gushing like the soda when the tab cracks open.

I wait for the beep.

"Um, my name is Alia and um, I was referred to you by a friend, and well, I just really need to get in to see you. Um, so I have a diagnosis of bipolar disorder and generalized anxiety and well, maybe other stuff too, um I don't know. But uh, my mom broke her back a few days ago and well, I'm just really tired because I'm her caregiver and this stress, well, I mean at night and sleep, well I just really need to get in to see about my medications and well, um, just could you call me back? I really need some help. Yeah, so could you just call me back?"

My voice hitches on the last few words and they come out breathy and strangled. I look up and my eyes meet Josh's. Tears spill down my cheeks. I married a man whose arms have held steady through my darkest nights and still I feel alone in the world. It's broken him, how unfixable I am.

Josh wraps his arms around my body and pulls me into him, and I come into his embrace; he rests his chin on the top of my head. I feel nothing at all. I am a carcass, carved out and bloodless. I feel godforsaken on the bad days. And the bad days are many. I carry my phone everywhere, constantly checking to make sure the ringer is on. I keep swiping at the screen, willing it to ring.

God promises to never leave or forsake me. I've written the reminders for days like this. Days when emptiness screeches in my ears and pounds in my head. The world is colorless again, the sounds are dull, my kids' laughter offers no joy. The sunshine makes my eyes hurt.

I am frantic and agitated and hollow all at once. I go through the motions of mothering my children and caring for my injured mom but find myself tucked into a corner of the couch by evening with my face buried in my hands, gasping and panting like I'm birthing a devil. The anxiety has settled in deep in my gut and it's pushing my lungs down into my spine. I am being crushed from the inside out.

How long, Oh Lord? Why do you hide your face from me? Why do you deny me your presence when I need you most?

I hear nothing. The phone sits mockingly silent. I feel as though God has hung up on me.

My seven-year-old wanders in with his arms full of stuffed animals. He plants a moose by my side, and Packy the elephant, and Slothy the sloth looks up from my lap with small, glassy eyes. I see my reflection in them. I am a woman whose child can sense a despair so thick and suffocating he feels the need to offer comfort in the only ways he knows how. Even my children try to fix me. But there is no remedy. No antidote to drink down, no easy answers.

It takes every ounce of energy to harness my cheek muscles and contort them into a smile that barely parts my lips and doesn't reach my eyes. My older kids would see through my facade, but my seven-year-old seems appeased. He climbs onto me and presses his cheek against mine before scampering off down the hall to play. At the entrance to the hallway, he glances back over his shoulder and flashes me a tentative look. My smile vanished as soon as he turned his back.

At my worst, I imagine they'd all be better off without me. In my darkest moments, I fear I've ruined them. I fear the cost of loving me is too great a price to ask anyone to pay.

I fear when I've taught them of the gospel, and God's strength made perfect in weakness, that what they've witnessed is God does not answer our prayers. I fear I've taught them of a Jesus I can no longer see or feel. I fear I am praying in the dark and it just echoes in a world devoid of God. I fear the good days were a hoax and the bad days are the reality.

Even on the good days I fear I'll get sucked back under, churned violently under the waves, like a spin cycle set to run too long, tumbling me in vicious circles.

I feared it when I was jubilant and every good thing was like low-hanging fruit, so ripe and easy to pluck from the branches, heavy with worth and promise.

I fear the fall. The cycle. Beginning again.

Sometimes hope terrifies me. I'm not supposed to say that. It seems contrary to all the good things we're taught.

Here's the funny thing, if such things could truly ever be funny: I trust God and have faith and then there's this too. This hesitancy to hope. How do we keep our native tongue when our lives are filled with unspeakable things? Things we cannot even wrap words around? I pray to the God of lost things and the God of found things, and I know he's one and the same. How that makes sense is still something I'm trying to figure out. I might not know it any better than this: he gives and he takes away; blessed be the name of the Lord.

God Gives Good Days

On the good days, I stoke the fire until it's fevered and snapping like the height of a jazz song, the heat caressing my skin like a lover, and I watch the snow fall outside. I don't fear these new beginnings when everything is blanketed and pure. And I can't crush the hope that rises from the embers.

On the good days, strawberries taste like sugar in my bowl. Nina Simone sings melodies straight to my hips and they sway with my womanhood, sensual and beautiful and feeling good. They don't feel like mama hips and the remnants of a birthing belly. I don't feel like damaged goods when there's extra wobbly bits. My hips are miracle makers; they disrupt everything I've seen in the glossy ads or the TV shows. I rebel against the befores and afters that promise I'll be more beautiful later, after I lose ten pounds or a hundred, or master that messy bun.

On the good days, I splash Ruby Woo red lipstick on my lips and sing, "Freedom is mine, and I know how I feel, it's a new dawn, it's a new day, it's a new life for me. I'm feeling good," along with Nina.[1] I believe her on the good days.

On the good days, my fingertips feel like angel wings, and they soar across the keyboard tapping a lifeline like Morse code to navigate my way back to God's goodness. My hand scribbles frantically in the margins of my notebook and on old receipts and the ink bleeds my story on every blank space, and I remember God's faithfulness to me. I am a woman called. On the good days, my offering makes sense and it doesn't feel like a catalog of brittle words strung together like gibberish. On the good days words come fast, like the burst of a blackberry on my tongue.

I speak my native tongue, the language of hope fluent in every word I pen.

On the good days I make my kids laugh, I dance in the kitchen, and my husband smiles at me with his boyish grin, seeing the girl he fell in love with. Our kids call us gross and roll their eyes, through smiles and giggles. On good days, I believe I am a woman loved. I am home.

On the good days, I set my face to the sun and let it bathe my cheekbones with hope. And it's no less scary, but it's everywhere and I can feel it as a tangible thing. I can feel it. Untethered hope as native to my skin and soul and body as the DNA encoded in my cells. I can't help but let it lead me toward spring. This hope is hereditary; I have inherited it and my descendants carry it with me.

On the Bad Days

But what lies beneath, often dormant, is my propensity for soul-wrecking depression. I am a magnet of opposite poles, afflicted with pressure and ripping me apart at my core. I fear hope as much as I fear despair. I live a life grappling for center.

Bipolar depression terrorizes my rhythm from my hips, and it rips song lyrics and laughter from my once-red lips. It leaves slippered feet stumbling on crumpled gray tarsals.

Once again, I'm shuffling Sisyphus's eternal burden up and down and back again, and instead of a crushing stone, I'm bearing the weight of a troubled mind, a life of mental illness, a broken body. And hope feels like the worst betrayal when the bad days come. Because God takes away.

When the bad days come, I remember my dreams long enough to know I was ridiculous to trust so blindly.

When the bad days come, I push my face into the pillow and silently scream. I thrash about in my body like a trapped animal longing to shed its skin, writhing in this world that never could fit. On the bad days I can't imagine good could come of any of this.

On the bad days, I hear the sorrowful notes in Nina's song and the pain tinged in her words. I listen to "Strange Fruit" and realize we haven't come far at all. The headlines declare the gross misdeeds of men, the rationale to hate, to fear, to "other" each other. I cannot stomach another person made in the image of God bled lifeless in the street, name hashtagged and retweeted while so many stay silent or unseeing of the injustice all around them. On the bad days, I see it in the pews, in the hands lifted to a God we forgot to trust, and a Lord we refuse to surrender to, all to make America something it never was—the great hope.

On the bad days, I have to summon up every ounce of energy in me to not scream in the faces of the well-meaning ones, "You don't understand! I don't want advice from your hypnotherapist or your CrossFit coach or a pamphlet on the miracle shake that your moody great-aunt drank and was cured. I don't want any pithy quotes about God using everything or just washing your face and getting on with it."

On the bad days, I want to shake with rage, like the madwoman I fear I am. Because don't you see? The energy to smile and nod and pretend I haven't tried every last thing makes me so exhausted I want to pound floorboards with balled fists and wail because there are so few safe places for the hurting to just hurt. The well-meaning ones peddle quick fixes and snake-oil tinctures that go down easy and come back violently.

What a catastrophe unbridled certainty can be when unleashed on the hurting.

On the bad days, my mirror tells me not to bother with seeing beauty because my skin isn't clear, my eyes slant narrow with suspicion, my lips strangle with broken sentences, my body sags with the gravity of bipolar tectonics, shifting my days to little earthquakes.

So many breakable things shatter around me.

On the bad days, I feel it's all wreckage, and the Richter scale measures Sisyphus's stone rolling back down just like I knew it would, demolishing everything in its path. I am the worst kind of fraud, one who hoped and lost it all so easily, so often.

On the really bad days, I'll do nothing but fail and fall short. I am certain I am a nuisance, a bother, a constant burden of misery. I'll believe my kids would be better off without me. How many times can a child watch his mother sink into despair and not be irreparably damaged? How many times will I fail them if I remain?

I'll imagine slipping quietly from the house, past the dishes and the vase of ranunculus on the table I bought during the descent to remind me of beauty. I'll walk down to the neck of water where the swirl of the river bends like it's sitting in the crook of God's finger and I'll let it strangle me. I'll end the misery for everyone. It'll all be very discreet, I tell myself. A hunter or a hiker or someone kayaking on the backlands will find me. There will be no mess to clean up, I wouldn't want to further burden anyone. I'll believe Josh will remarry; I'll write him a letter beforehand, give him my permission, release him from loving me. She'll be healthy, someone slightly younger and full of vibrancy, someone who doesn't carry so much sadness behind her eyes. Someone who will surf with him and be kind to our kids. Someone who doesn't require so much care.

On the very bad days, I confess my doubt to the emptiness and hope that in the midst of the silence, God will hear me. I pray, "I believe, help my unbelief." I pray it like a mantra to calm and center me.

Searching for a Savior

I don't want to suffer anymore. But I must survive. So I ask for help. I ask for it all the time. My God, why is this so hard? Why is asking for help so impossible in our culture? But I already know why. It's because we cannot admit how much we truly need, how desperate we really are, how dark the world sometimes gets. There are so few safe spaces to admit how bad the bad days are. We don't want pity, we don't want attention, we just want to not hurt anymore. No one can imagine the strength it takes to admit how weak you are.

I promise those I love and who love me that I will never stop asking for help on the bad days, even though it pains me to do it. It's a promise I can't afford to break because so often the prettily packaged antidote is the poison that vows that this can all be over. You won't hurt or hurt people anymore. You won't be a burden to everyone. You won't have to bear witness to a savage and vulgar world you feel powerless to change.

It's packaged like salvation, but I've written the reminders and read God's Word and I know salvation is my Jesus.

I unravel the pretty package until all that's left is me as undone as the woman who wept and worshiped at Jesus's feet. I am a scandalous woman who unravels her hair in public among good company and the lookers-on, wild and tangled and unwashed; I offer the only thing I have: my whole-broken self. *Remind me of the true things, Lord.* And I wait.

This is the only faith I know. The doubt and the waiting to hear. The belief that my salvation has come. So I wait by the phone.

It's difficult to feel God's love when it seems he's abandoned you and you're suffering. I've lived a life of questions: Where is God when I hurt? How can God be good and allow bad things to happen? Does God see me? Does God love me?

I'm desperate for Christ's presence and beginning to understand more of what it means to be poor in spirit. A longing so tangible it aches for just a touch, a glimpse, a taste. I am an unclean woman grasping at the hem of his garment. I am desperate at the well with lips cracked like the face of the desert and a thirst so strong from choking on dust.

I am hungry eyes in search of the kingdom of heaven, ravenous desire and such a keen awareness of all I lack on my own.

This is not the woman I could be. This is not my full potential with my God-given gifts and talents and passion. I could do so much for God if I could just stay well. If I could just be healed. If I wasn't broken in the first place.

The Beginning of Hope

In February of 2016, during a period when I was doing well mentally and physically and there were more good days than bad ones, I saw a link on a friend's Facebook page for an Author's Retreat for People of Color that was local to me. The retreat intrigued me, and I signed up for it.

I sent in a standard bio and a headshot and forgot about it. I didn't know anyone attending, but I reached out to a few friends to see if they were interested and could make it. They couldn't.

A couple weeks later, I got the email roster of attendees, and I did what anyone who is anxiety prone would do: I googled a few of them. And then that familiar voice rose up from the broken parts, like white-hot shame: *You don't belong there.* I imagined circles of influence, and they were the circles of my childhood. Because these were real leaders; these were educated, passionate people changing their neighborhoods, their churches, their justice systems, and the world around them. These were people who could explain their answers.

I am an overweight, mentally ill high-school dropout, well acquainted with financial hardship and lack, who writes her feelings on the internet and sometimes struggles with suicidal ideation. I can't even remember to put the laundry from the washer into the dryer without having to rerun it a few times. How could I possibly have anything to contribute?

So I reached out to safe people, writer friends who get me, and I let the doubt and fear and insecurity tumble out. Sometimes, despite everything, I am really bad at asking for help. I just limp along and pretend it hasn't derailed me at times, this fear that I am not enough. Because I know all the hollow places, my lack. My friends prayed for me and among them came a single comment:

> Listening to your "rant" was really listening to something needed and prophetic. You are in no way an imposter and your voice and eyes are needed.

And then I did what I do. I cried off all my makeup. I didn't know how much I needed to be told, *You have a right to be there too.* I've learned that I can't always trust my emotions—mental illness makes them jagged and skewed and they cut right through me on the bad days. I've learned to seek out credible voices that dull the edges of those sharp feelings.

I talked myself into going. I convinced myself it would be fine. They were all writers, we're usually messy people. We are all Christians; this isn't middle school all over again. But the night I was supposed to go, I realized my mom accidentally took my keys. I was left stranded—knowing that by the time I made it there, everyone would already have met and been together and I would walk in late and alone. On the outside.

It would be another circle to stand at the margins of and hope there was room for me.

But I've been taken out on so many days. I've had my choices removed because there are days when I simply cannot do anything but survive. Days when the agony seems to win and my body fails and my thoughts spiral and all I can do is pray for mercy, pray for rescue. This instead was a good day. This was me able, but not wanting to because of insecurity. I went back and read the comments. I echoed their prayers for me and fought back the anxiety.

I went. And when we gathered in a circle, I stuffed myself into the corner of a couch and silently cursed myself for having gone. As introductions were made and each person spoke, I shrunk down smaller and smaller. Having thumbed through the retreat program on arrival and seeing everyone's colorful bios with degrees and accolades and ministries, all professional and glossy, I realized that I had literally written something about making my home in Central Oregon with chickens and a bunny and something about homeschooling kids and making googly-eyes at my husband. That last part about the googly-eyes didn't make it into the program, and

I can only think it was a kind soul who edited it out or God who allowed that part to be accidentally cut. You guys, I cannot make this stuff up.

When it got to me, I literally said I basically write my feelings on the internet and am not really sure what I'm doing there and then I babbled. I have no idea what I said. None. My mouth continued on like it was possessed by some foreign control center spewing out excuses for my existence in total disregard of my brain. Everyone was kind and generous. It almost made it worse.

I went home and Josh asked how it went. I told him I died of humiliation, have no place there, and will never send a bio anywhere ever again. *I don't belong,* I whispered. *I have nothing to say, these people are doing the real work.*

I decided I must have been hallucinating to believe my story matters. I am a woman with no résumé, no qualifications. I am not a leader; most days I can barely stand. Some days I cannot even get out of bed or run a brush through my hair. And my lack, my weakness felt like the deepest sorrow, like an ever-widening gap that would swallow me whole.

Write the Reminders

Josh asked if I was going back the next day. If there were any way I could've not gone back, I would have. But this retreat was put on by people from my old church. They would ask how it went. I'd have to make up a reason why I didn't return.

I decided to go, but I began imagining fake emergencies that would suddenly call me home if I felt like I was going to die on the spot.

Josh, who is good to me, tells me to make a file with read-ers' emails and the comments that say, "I feel less alone now," or "You make me see the goodness of God, even now when it hurts so much," and to read them when I have nothing to offer, and that doesn't seem like enough.

So after I hyperventilated on the couch and sobbed and told him I don't know if I can do the things that make me come alive because being fully alive and fully myself is the most vulnerable and scary place of all, after I curled in a ball and he stroked my hair and I said all the desperate things one more time, he said to write the reminders. The altars to remember. He didn't say it in those words because I'm the writer and he's mostly quiet and words aren't his thing, but that was basically it. Remember.

The next morning I woke up early to write when the sky was black as pitch, and I pulled back the blinds to watch the sun rise over my laptop. When the light broke, I saw that Josh had written *You're Good Enough* in window marker from the outside before he left for work.

I've known I wanted to write books someday, but know-ing the destination doesn't mean the journey is any easier. I've said *no* and *it's not time* for years. I said I would know when it was. I didn't want to put down words I haven't car-ried with me for some time. I don't want to fill the pages with premature stories so I can have my name on a shelf. I know too many published authors to believe this is any kind of holy-grail achievement or that I will somehow be "good enough" with my book for sale on Amazon. If anything, the writers I know have an even bigger crisis of worth once you can be evaluated by book sales and stars on Amazon. It's not easy to get published, but it's even harder for a person of color to get published in the Christian market because it's a very white-dominant industry. But I was finally feeling it may be time to write my story. I could feel God prompting me, but I was still scared. I thought the retreat might help me learn how to navigate some of the obstacles inherent in publishing that are specific to people of color.

I drove to the second day of the Author's Retreat while using the Voxer app on my phone to send a writing friend a long message about dreams and dream-breakers. I knew my destination, but the journey terrified me. She agreed bipolar is a beast. Dreams are hard to hold on to. Staying fluent in hope is no small thing. Sometimes surviving sucks the hopeful syllables right out of my throat.

I could feel the tension in my shoulders, like corded bundles tightening up around my ears, as I climbed the stairs to the retreat. I poured hot water into a container of gluten-free oatmeal and let it simmer while I found a seat.

I asked one of the attendees how she slept, how was the jet lag. And then suddenly I was explaining how intimidated I was the night before, and how I felt so awkward because I didn't know this retreat was for "real" leaders and educated people, not just random people who write on the internet.

It just came tumbling out, rolling up through my tension, and suddenly it was spilling from my lips like I had just burped up something unpleasant. I felt I needed to apologize for being there. I wished I could stop and take a huge inhale, sucking those words back from the space where they were floating between us when she chimed in with, "Oh, me too. I totally felt that way too." And then she shared her story, the one she was also holding in, and I heard every single word as if it were my own.

The tension eased in my neck and I breathed a little deeper in my lungs. I'm not the only one. Our honesty is an invitation. Our weakness makes space. Reminder one. *Thank you, Lord.*

A Prophet with a Spreadsheet

During the first session, Al Hsu, senior editor at Intervarsity Press, shared a presentation on "The Publishing World: Trends, Context, and Where You Fit." Where I fit? But I'm the girl who doesn't fit. I'm the girl who doesn't belong.

Sometimes God sends us prophets. They're just doing their work. They're doing what they were made to do, same as any other day. And they're oblivious to the places God prepared ahead of time, but on that day, they speak hope into your weary, shame-filled places. On that day, their words open places to dream again, to find the wings God was shaping all those painful times you were plunged into the fire. On that day, they showed up to do work they excel at, but it's more than a job, it's a ministry, and they have no idea what their obedience to their one thing has done for someone else. They help silence the voices and remind you who God is.

I'd never heard an Asian American address issues specific to me. Specific to shame and culture, and wanting to do the work but not knowing how to get past the hurdles that keep me silent and strangled. When he started sharing the Where I Fit portion, I could feel my eyes get watery and I stared at my laptop screen blinking furiously. I would not ugly cry in the middle of this session! There are limits to my humility, people, and ugly crying in the middle of a session on publishing trends was where I drew the line!

God was reaching into the tension, into the places where I've believed I wasn't good enough. Where I continue to forget he has made me good because he is good. My shoulders melted down into the whole of me. I was breathing all the way down to my gut.

The weekend continued, and in tiny pockets of conversation, I began to see how each person was doing their work—holy, important things in both big and small spaces. How everyone wrestled with bringing their voice in one way or another. How everyone had barriers to opportunity or oppression. No one had a cleared path to do the thing God was calling them to. Everyone was battling something. I heard my voice unfiltered, and although we all came with different goals and various obstacles, I started to believe I had a story not just worth telling but worth hearing. Al Hsu said, "No book is for everybody, but every book is for somebody."[2]

Somehow I'd forgotten about my somebodies. I'd forgotten about the people who need space to believe God is still good. Even when I'm crushed with despair, even when my body fails, even when my kids have needs I cannot meet. Even when I have more questions than answers and my faith feels like stumbling around in the dark, God is still good. I'd forgotten about the people who need to know that the way they see the world isn't the only way to see the world and that maybe we could all learn something by listening better. I'd forgotten about the people who need to know the weak will be made strong.

I'd forgotten how often I write the reminders for times when the world goes dark and the bad days come and I'd read those words back like they were a foreign language—something I used to be fluent in but had grown rusty. I'd sound out the syllables. I'd trace under the words with my finger and it would slowly come back to me, the phonics of hope, something about the God who comes for me again and again. The God of the lost and found.

I'd remember how God still moves in the scorched land, in the bruised and busted-up parts, in the lack and the weakness and the never enough, in the halves of me that never seem to add up to a whole: God still redeems.

Sometimes it looks like ordinary. Sometimes it looks like miracle. I believe it is both. I'd forgotten how in telling our stories we don't just relate to each other; we belong to each other. I am not alone. And neither are you.

To Hope or Not to Hope

After that retreat, the words came quicker, filling notebooks and Word docs. It had been over a year since I had taken the editor's card at the JumpingTandem retreat. The message I had spoken continued to be refined through trial after trial. My weakness made strong in Christ.

I reached out to Rebekah, the editor, on April 4, 2016, to ask some questions about publishing. I finally felt it was time to move ahead with pursuing this book. I had started to work on my book proposal, the first step to getting a book deal with a traditional publisher. It's a long process of fleshing out the message of the book, the intended reader, the market, and of course, why you're qualified to write it. She was gracious to answer my questions and offered to look at my proposal when I was done. My heart was bolstered—finally all the years of being poor, and broken, and weak would have their purpose in the culmination of this message.

Exactly seven days after I emailed Rebekah, my mother broke her back in our yard and I found her. I was her only caretaker.

A few days after that I left my message on a psychiatrist's answering service hoping to be seen because I was experiencing the worst mixed bipolar state I had ever had.

Waiting by the phone for an answer, I was a shell of that woman who believed she could write a book, hollowed out and cradling my wounds. How could this be what God wanted for me? Why let me be inspired, let me hope, only to crush me again?

I thought, *How can I bring God glory when I can't even mother my own children well? When I can't care for my broken mother without losing my mind? How can I serve the church, my husband, our family, the world? How can I write of God's faithfulness if he won't hold still and just be faithful? How can I do anything at all that's pleasing to God if I am so poor in spirit? So completely unable and lacking in every way.*

There's pressure to be more and do more, and we've all felt it, whether you struggle with mental illness or not. That slow, churning ache that our "one wild and precious life"[3] is slipping away and we've done nothing to make it matter. I've woken panicked that my life will be wasted because I wasn't paying attention or doing enough. Because I wasn't strong enough to count, to make a dent on this busted-up world of ours.

I've feared I'd make it into heaven, but just barely, and while everyone else was getting their crowns and congratulatory "well done, my good and faithful servants" from God, I would be at the back of the crowd shuffling my feet and trying not to say anything stupid that would get me kicked out.

I've feared I didn't measure up. That I wasn't strong enough or smart enough or pretty enough. But even when my skin was smooth like marble, and my body was strong and young, and I was cute-store-sized, even when my mind was clearer, I wasn't enough then either.

I cannot remember the days when I swung into the sky with my brown skinned knees pumping hard and my tennis shoes stretched to the heavens to see if I could topple the swing set. I cannot remember what it felt like to believe I could fly.

I cannot remember the days when the fruit grew wild around us and I walked in the cool of evening, childlike and unashamed. Known and seen and beloved. I cannot remember freedom at all.

Some hope fades with age, clouded out with responsibilities and duty, grown-up life where our monsters are now finances, health, marriage problems, and depression.

Some of us stopped dreaming so young, when doors crept open and real shadow monsters stood. The place where nightmares live full grown in our memories. Some of us were no longer naked and unashamed.

Some of us stopped believing when we hit the ground one too many times, and we knew then and there that we had no wings to fly, only torn skin on our knees and flesh on our bones, the taste of blood on our teeth. And all of it hurt. And somewhere along the line, the stories we told ourselves were less about redemption and more about obstacles. Less about sovereignty and more about survival. And we put the childish things away, like faith and hope, dreams and won-

der. Somewhere along the line many of us got realistic about
what faith looked like in our new world, and it became trying harder and doing more. It became tired and sad and just
out of reach.

Sometimes I try to hold on tighter, to pray a more eloquent
prayer confessing all the right faith instead of admitting I
come once again doubting, once again needing to be helped
along in my belief. Sometimes I try to battle my fears with
reason, hoping to flood the anxiety and sadness like snuff-
ing a smoldering wick set to spark again any moment. I
keep looking over my shoulder, watching for the despair
that hangs on the hems of my days, dragging its claws up
my spine.

All this looking out left me even more depleted. I cannot
build a fortress tall enough or strong enough to keep my
own flesh at bay. There is no fight left in me. Only surrender.

What does it take to keep the language of hope fluent
on your tongue when all you taste is despair and the ash of
burnt offerings you never imagine setting on the altar in the
first place?

Maybe all it takes is relenting to our vast and unavoidable
need. Maybe when I worship with both hands empty and
the tears flowing down, it is not the praise of a madwoman
but one utterly desperate for him. And maybe that is the gift
of suffering, the gift of weakness, of being poor in spirit.
Maybe being poor in spirit is the invitation to truly see the
kingdom of God as one who is so loved, so valuable, so recognized by Jesus, a person can come reeking with need and
not be found wanting.

I meet God most often while splayed not on the altar of
my offering but of my poverty. The threshold of despair for

things I cannot produce or manufacture with my own soiled hands, my own dreadful will, my own can-do attitude is an entrance to mercy. I find God in a life never lacking a certain quiet desperation.

So I wait for God to pick up. I'm waiting for my Jesus to say, "Your faith has saved you; go in peace."

A Risen Savior

I set my face to that spot in the sky where the light will rise and believe in morning. I set my life to the sunrise, knowing it has never failed. I believe in the steadying grace of new light, and although I grieve the darkest nights, as long and constant as they seem, I have set my hope in the infallibility of risen things that come like ransom. A Savior, a dream, and a great, wild, terrifying hope. Remember. You have written the reminders for just such a time as this. You have seen God. Bear witness.

The God of found things who sees me, who comes for me, again and again. He is the God of the lost coin, he is the God who would leave an entire flock of healthy and profitable sheep for that one lost, broken lamb. He is the God of the lost and I will find myself once again in him. *Jesus, come for me*, I cry out.

I remember small grace and grasp hold, naked and nothing, and I worship Who I cannot even feel.

Isn't this faith? Not that we wouldn't fear, or doubt, or suffer. Not that the bad days wouldn't come, sometimes unrelenting, sometimes often. Faith doesn't eliminate feeling wrecked or salvaged by the good days or bad days, but the stone isn't being rolled up and crashing down like some mythical tragedy of lessons to be learned. No, the stone's been rolled away; the risen things take their place in the souls of mortals and we call them hope. Our only hope. And so I wait for God to answer me.

> Then Job arose and tore his robe and shaved his head and fell on the ground and worshiped. And he said, "Naked I came from my mother's womb, and naked I shall return. The LORD gave, and the LORD has taken away; blessed be the name of the LORD." (Job 1:20–21)

And then the phone rings, and the kind voice on the other end says, "Alia? I got your call. I have a space open for you."

I am not alone in the world. Jesus comes for me again and again.

Part 4

glory

eleven

And If Not, He Is Still Good

The Glory of the Beloved

My deepest awareness of myself is that I
am deeply loved by Jesus Christ and I have
done nothing to earn it or deserve it.

BRENNAN MANNING

There are branches missing from my family tree. I remember
sitting at our kitchen table with a printed handout from Judah's kindergarten class, a sturdy trunk split evenly on each
side like a balanced scale with lines for each family member.

Judah held his pencil balled up in his chubby little fist
and painstakingly wrote Alia and Josh in the slots for mom
and dad. For aunts and uncles, he wrote Sarah and Jordan
on my side, and Anna on the other. He filled in his grandparents, Amaji and Papaji on my side and Grandma Ruth

and Grandpa Dave on the other, and then he'd point to the slots on his dad's side, and I'd spell out the names, Great-Grandpa Harry and Great-Grandma Dorothy. But when he'd point to mine, I'd mostly shake my head. I don't know their names. I don't know them. And when he was finished, the tree was hopelessly lopsided. There were so many gaps. So much missing history.

Family trees are complicated. Some are so full you can barely cram the names on the page and they start to climb the sides of the paper, like they're sprouting new limbs. I have friends who can trace their ancestors all the way to the boats that first brought them across the sea. Other family trees have been chopped down short, branches severed, roots dug up.

I don't know why teachers assign these. There are so many ways we don't fit in tidy slots. So many ways our roots are just as hard to explain as our growth. Because our growth is seldom linear, seldom so easily charted and mapped out. Many times, it is us, circumnavigating the world in a dinghy that takes on water. Our universe tilts on its axis, spins us wildly about.

Dust to Dust

My ancestors have no graves. At least not that I know of. Only ashes, burnt down to dust in flames, ancient bones to rubble.

After my grandma died, we drove along the switchbacks of Highway 536, gliding easily along the watermelon-hued backdrop of the Sandia Mountains, and found a bluff overlooking a serene scene. I remember trees and a view of a modest canyon, but nothing spectacular. Nowhere I'd want to spend eternity. There is no way I'd ever be able to find my way back there and maybe it was okay that none of us ever tried.

We had a simple box with her remains and her name written along the top. Helene Havens. But we only called her Grandma Skippy. I don't think I ever asked her why. Where had that nickname come from? By the time I knew her, maybe she wouldn't have remembered anyway.

The box was cardboard, like a small present you might get in the mail with a toy inside. I stood with my back to the wind, but my mom faced it head-on, and I can remember she didn't cry as she opened it and we each took a handful of ash. I remember thinking I'd cry if my mother died, but maybe it was different for grown-ups. Or maybe she spent her tears in secret.

The ashes weren't dusty like I'd expected. Not like the ash left over after our campfire had burned down to powder during one of my dad's impromptu camping trips.

We'd sit by the campfire and my dad would enthrall us with his stories while my mom prepared fried rice or chili in a giant wok. Our marshmallows turned into tiny torches, crisping into balls of gooey charcoal before plopping into the flames, and our fingers and faces were sticky from the few that made it to our mouths. Once, I tried to grab the burned-to-a-crisp marshmallow off too soon and the center oozed out and burned my fingers, blistering my skin.

I thought about the feel of that burn as I held my grandma's ashes, and even though I know she couldn't feel anything, I hated the thought of it. Her ashes were coarse and hard, like tiny pebbles, the color and weight of kitty litter.

I held my fist up and let my fingers open on my palm like a budding flower, the wind catching the ashes and carrying them like dandelion seeds over the canyon. And just like that, she was gone. In a way, it was a small mercy. She had been disappearing one memory at a time, one moment. And she was afraid. The world was no longer familiar, her body was tired, her mind confused. I loosened my grip all the way and she was carried into eternity, my hand once again ashen.

You Can't Die Out There

My dad's remains are in my mom's closet down the hall on the shelf. The box is bigger, and I wonder if it's because he was bigger than my tiny Asian grandmother. I don't know how these things work, but there's some sort of container inside and maybe that's what is taking up the space. When we went to the funeral home, the director opened a glossy pamphlet and my mom and I chose the most basic options. My dad would've hated being cooped up. Someday, we hope to scatter some of his ashes in India. He wanted to die there, where my parents had lived as missionaries for over a decade, but I didn't let him. I refused him the peace of anonymity, of knowing we would not bear witness to his deteriorating form, to bear witness to his death.

In India, when his mouth filled with blood and it poured from his throat, my mom called a friend who helped steer him down the stairs of their flat to get him to the hospital in Pune.

The phone call came and I don't remember the words on the other end of the line—the connection sounded like it was coming from another galaxy. This might be it. This might be goodbye, a spotty call from what might as well have been a million miles away.

If they couldn't cauterize the vessels in his esophagus, broken open from the pressure in his portal vein resulting from his failing liver, he would die in a hospital room with only my mom by his side. I had no current passport or visa, no money to buy a plane ticket. No choices. I stayed by the phone back in those days when you had no choice but to be tethered to land.

I wondered about all of the unsaid things. My dad was my hero when I was a girl, but he'd morphed into a man as I aged. He became flawed. He became human and at times, I hated him for it. It felt like a betrayal when I saw he was just a man, with raw blood in his veins and the ability to disappoint. The stories became flimsier, because I knew the man he was when he wasn't leading, when he wasn't teaching or telling stories, when he wasn't dreaming up some grand scheme. I saw where he was sick and dying, where he was mortal. Where he could be wounded, where he could wound.

It'd been years since I'd hidden in my room at night reading my Bible in secret so my dad wouldn't get the upper hand because I joined his side of things—just like he'd said I would.

We'd made peace, a sort of surrender to the ways things had gone wrong for us, after I gave birth to my oldest son, Judah. I remember being flat on my back with the blue curtain propped up between my breasts and my abdomen, sectioning me off so I wouldn't see myself splayed open as the doctor cut my child from my body. And when I heard him squeal and Josh brought him around to show me, he tipped his arm forward in a bow, revealing our tiny baby in a pink-and-blue knit cap and swaddled body.

I cried, "Please take him, I can't! I can't take him!" For those few seconds I would have gladly given him to any nice family who promised to love him and raise him right, so complete was my fear that I was inadequate.

I was terrified I would drop him on the floor; my arms were still shaking and I could barely turn my head. My vision was a blur and I had a flood of terror so strong it felt like a physical wave, a wash of heat cascading over me from my skull to my rib cage, where it faded into numbness from the anesthesia. It was that old familiar voice whispering, "Who do you think you are mothering a child? You can't even birth a baby."

I had been diagnosed with preeclampsia and my doctor decided our best option was to induce me at thirty-seven weeks. After twenty-seven hours of labor, I'd failed. My body erupted in fever, I trembled and vomited and they were saying they must take him now. They rushed me into surgery. They gutted me, pulling him from between my hips, and even though I couldn't feel a thing, I still felt like I was being ripped open. So when I saw his face, when our eyes connected only minutes later, it was as if he could see inside me. As if he knew I could not do this. I could not mother him.

Later, in the recovery room, when he drew back and his face pinched up in resentment as he struggled to take my breast but could not latch, I knew I had already failed him. I had failed him before I had ever conceived. A night that should have been celebration was filled with sorrow and regret. I realized that no matter how much I loved my boy, I would fail him. I had no choice but to fail him.

It offered me the tiniest glimpse into the fear of a parent, to the leap it takes to love another person with such ferocity that no matter your intentions, you are destined to screw it up.

The next morning, I unswaddled Judah and took in his tiny toes, his red legs still curled fetal across his diapered bottom. I unfolded him and let my eyes gorge on the beauty of my son. I picked him up in nothing but his fresh skin, pressed him to my bare chest, and lowered my nose to his head—smelling the soft cap of downy baby fluff. In that moment I felt my whole body contract, pulling myself back together, rhythmically adding another ring to my trunk. I realized then how much my dad had always loved me, how hard he'd tried to hold us all together.

Later, when my parents came to meet their first grand-child, I looked at my dad through teary eyes and passed Judah to his familiar arms, with the menacing butterfly tat-too. He looked down and his eyes filled too as if he was saying, *Yes, Alia, I know. I know. I love you just like this.*

And I realized how hard he tried. How we try to be strong for our kids, how sometimes we try to be everything to every-one, and we fail because we were never meant for that kind of glory, that kind of heroism. Over time, we become known, and this is hard. Because when we're known, when we're seen, there's a reckoning. Do we love the inglorious bits? Do we love the reality? Do we love enough to weather weakness?

I forgave him that day in the hospital. Not all at once, for forgiveness isn't immediate, and I had the deep scars of a girl whose daddy seemed to forget her in those teen years when his eyes were so fixed on her brother. When keeping him alive and on the right path took up so much of my dad's attention that he all but forgot he had a girl who adored him. Maybe it was a sort of seesaw—I was a dying girl first while my brother looked on and then it was my brother's turn to come back from the grave. Maybe it was just hard to keep fighting death? But I forgave my dad all the same, in increments over time. I allowed my dad his weakness because I felt my own. Only I didn't speak those words aloud. I didn't tell him.

So when I wait by the phone to hear if I will ever be able to tell him, I think of this. Of vulnerability and saying what we mean. Of forgiveness and grace, weakness and wonder. Of death and birth and the new life that comes from both. I wait to see if I can say goodbye.

Attending Weakness

My dad didn't die in a hospital in India. He died in hospice, almost four years after he had his first esophageal bleed. He died a few feet away from my mom and me, who sat clutching each other on the couch. My parents left India because I petitioned them to let us help shoulder the burden of his care. I couldn't imagine my dad dying so far away with no way to get to him. No way to stand with my mom and hold her hand in mine and tell her I was there for her. No way to be strong for them both.

In my father's last days, his hunger vanished. As he shrunk like a hollowed-out husk, his spirit being gathered by the very hand of God, his appetites died within him. The hospice nurse handed me a pamphlet about the stages of death and closed her palm gently over the back of my hand. It said your loved one may lose their appetite and have no need for fluids or foods at this point. Their body is conserving energy for the end-of-life changes that are occurring. They may be going through emotional and spiritual changes as their body focuses on the task before them. An IV might be necessary for your loved one's comfort. Loss of appetite is one of the final stages of death.

Skilled hands slipped on latex gloves and threaded an IV into his veins to keep him hydrated and to limit pain, but his lips had already spoken their last words and eaten their last bites. His eyes never opened again once the ambulance arrived to maneuver him down the steps of our house and on to hospice for his final days.

I knew my dad was dying long before his body actually failed. His personality was siphoned off slowly at first; he'd find himself confused or muddy brained. He would sometimes act like a child, irrational and upset about things. He'd get irritated with my children, and sometimes I'd have to settle disputes between them like he was one of their siblings instead of their grandfather. He lost context and told stories that no longer made much sense. Some part of himself still recognized all he was losing, all he had lost, and he retreated into himself. He was no longer loud and gregarious. He no longer wanted to entertain company. He no longer required an audience. This was the hardest part to endure. To watch the man I adored, the man I had made peace with as human, be so very human. So very frail and broken and hurting. So incredibly weak.

He could no longer feed himself or make it to the bathroom on his own. One day, before he was unable to move on his own, he fell in the shower while Josh was at work. I backed into the bathroom, covering him with a towel while my mom and I strained to lift him up and out. He was shivering like a child, crying in my arms.

I've never known such a desperate weakness. Such a deliberate pain as losing yourself completely. Mind and body and soul.

In hospice, he slipped easily from consciousness into a hushed body I no longer recognized as my dad. I didn't know my dad without his appetite for life. Without his taste for loud music, James Taylor or the Traveling Wilburys on vinyl. Without his quick wit and the ability to make everyone in the room laugh at one of his jokes. Without his stories.

When I was a girl, he would hoist me onto his lap and offer me love straight from his plate. He taught me that to offer a seat at a table was to invite communion and community.

He sat on mud floors in dung huts beneath the Himalayas scraping small handfuls of dahl and rice into his mouth, eating hot momos cooked in the hammered pot full of sizzling oil that spit and hissed on the open flames.

He held the white cardboard cone with frites and fritesaus, each bite warming me as we walked hand in hand from the street vendor in Holland. He ate oxtail soup and kimchi and lau lau in Hawaii. He scooped up menudo and posole with our Mexican friends. He ordered lengua tacos from the tiny taco stands and doused them with fiery hot peppers.

People always made room for him at their table. His fair skin and blue eyes were readily invited into so many cultures because of his love and respect for others' customs and foods. For his humility to sit and be a guest. They welcomed him because he truly appreciated the great wide world of tastes and flavors, the halo of fragrance from steaming pots and sizzling pans.

I remember once, before my dad's worsening health, I was awaiting my parents' arrival. They had flown into California from India and were driving up to Oregon to stay with us while on sabbatical. When hours had passed, I began to worry. I came to find out they'd met an Indian man and his family at a convenience store and got to talking. In the end, the man invited my parents to their house for tea and to see their garden. They offered my parents clippings of Indian herbs and spices to take home with them. No one remained a stranger when my dad was around.

He was happiest sharing a meal because a meal shared meant an open invitation to belong to each other.

But his hunger was no longer for this world. I watched sober eyed as my dad slipped from his body into eternity.

The hospital bed looked garish and oversized with his shrunken torso. The edema swelled his belly, feigning a fullness he could no longer get from food, and in those days it deflated like a balloon steadily losing air. His body sagged in dying, like the very soul of him had leaked out bit by bit.

And this was just one more part of it. This exhale where his body couldn't contain him anymore. He was letting go of this world as God called him home, and releasing his appetite was one of the final tethers that broke.

I didn't cry after my dad passed away. At least not right away. In all honesty, I felt a flood of relief as we sat watching. None of us imagined he would live as long as he did. By the time we were gathered around him in hospice, we were ready to let him go because he had suffered for so long. Because at that moment, we could only deal with the reality of his medications, his mind shrouded by disease, his constant pain, and his longing for heaven. He finally slipped from us that night, but he had been leaving us for years.

The nurse leaned over his hospice bed, cold stethoscope pressed to his chest, not needing to be warmed first. His breathing had been labored and rattly, then shallow, then silent.

My mom and I sat, sides touching on the couch, and the nurse rose, draped her stethoscope back around her neck, and shook her head slightly. Her voice was gentle and consoling, telling us what we already knew. My mom laced her hand in mine, tucked her head to my chest, and let out the tiniest muffled sob. She poured herself into me like I was the mother and she was my child. Her whimper shattered my heart, but I didn't weep with her. Not then.

I had already spent my tears the day my dad went to hospice and I dropped my mom off with him. I promised to return later that evening after I ran home and made dinner for my kids. I went upstairs to my parents' room and knew that the portable toilet and walker, the maroon sweatshirt he wore that was draped on his chair, the scrapbook I had made for him in his final weeks, these remnants of him would all need to be sorted or discarded. I wanted to remove the medical equipment before my mom came home because I knew how hard it was to lose someone and be left with the reminders. I still remembered the baby car seat and the onesies I had returned home to after I miscarried years ago. How the sight of them broke me open all over again. But I couldn't move. I stood in the doorway, doubled over, and wept. I had the sudden realization that he was never coming home. We'd never listen to another James Taylor song like we did when I was a girl. Me, riding shotgun, windows rolled down, lapping up air like a spaniel while singing along. My dad was gone.

After he died, it was all very businesslike. The nurses left us. We called Jordan to come before they took his body away. We stood in a half circle around him. I stared at his hands. His hands were the only part of him that still looked like my dad.

This was not the glorious death of a martyr, like the missionary biographies we read when we were little. It was not the saintly surrender of the strong and faithful. My dad died slowly, painfully, his humanity on display in ways that were undignified. He did not die with a chorus of angels singing, or at least not that we could hear. His last words were mumbled incoherently as were most of the words before that and before that.

And in the end, we let him go because we had so little left to hold on to.

I often wonder about those who remained at the foot of the cross to bear witness to Christ's death. Jesus's mother and Mary Magdalene, the soldiers, the priests, the disciples, and the crowd of spectators. Did they think Jesus strong for enduring or did they think him too weak to save himself? Did they watch death win and worry that it was all for naught? Did they wail and grieve and question how or why God forsook them? Jesus died an undignified death in abject pain, weakness, and humiliation, and I'm certain the world felt dark and silent, adrift in the storm with no anchor.

What Glory Remains for Us Mortals?

If you've ever felt lost at sea, like you are going in circles, in cycles, in seasons, it's probably because you are. I wondered in the writing of this book, in the decisions of which stories to tell, if it would seem redundant. This carnal yet sacred journey between trust and doubt, belief and unbelief, life and death, knowing God intimately and also wondering where he is when I'm bailing water on my dinghy while a tsunami warning blares.

I've been shipwrecked for glory, I thought, and that's okay. Just give me Jesus. "I'll lose it all if it means being close to you," I prayed. And when I flip back through the pages of my life, I see it again and again. That X marked out for me, when my world goes sideways, it looks like the cross. It is the goodness of God poured out before me in places no one would expect it. God's always been there. So often when the world feels like the harshest truth we go quiet. We don't want to admit we went down with the ship. We don't want to confess we are clinging to debris afloat in a sea of nothing but our losses.

But we are a beacon of hope for others who've lost their way. We share our stories and are vulnerable not because we wish to make an exhibition of our failures, our messy houses, our chaotic minds, our broken places, or our soiled linens. Vulnerability isn't just no-makeup selfies, or letting someone see our piles of laundry or dirty floors. True vulnerability is a confession of the places where we doubt, the places where we're not sure God is going to heal or touch or show up—the places we worry will always remain a little too broken, a little too human, a little too frail for polite company and pristine Sunday mornings. It's admittance that on our own we are lacking, desperate, and in need. True vulnerability says, "I believe, help my unbelief," and goes on to tell the story of how, if we're honest, we all reach our fingertips toward hope, grasping for a hem to make us whole again.

I've wondered if the end won't tie up as neatly as some hope. Maybe these things are true. Yet, so many of us live a life of sacred rhythms in the liminal space between hope and doubt. Day easing its burdens into the cool dark of night, sun slipping lazily in the sky. And darkness giving way to dawn break and the rising hope of new mornings. Chubby newborn thighs and the dying hands of a man too young to be lost in such ways.

There is a grief that lingers, that pops up with tears brimming at the sight of the oysters on sale in the crumpled Thanksgiving flyer. The oysters my dad loved. Or at the GIF of the elephant wearing pants he might have sent in an email had he stumbled across it first. He would have gotten a kick out of that and shared it with me. I could see it becoming his avatar. I would've rolled my eyes and smiled.

It might have become one of our inside jokes. We had many. One line and all of us would be howling with laughter, heads tipped back with abandon. We had history. And history and humor make for good memories. Sometimes grief is a smile as we remember and sometimes it is tears. There is room enough for both.

Growing toward Glory

Are any of us really so different from the disciples? How often will we see the face of God in our midst, the miracles, the hand of our Savior reaching toward us in the squall, ransoming us, the stone rolled away, the bread and wine still fresh on our tongues, and still we forget. I am three rooster crows cackling in the wind before I remember what it is to know Jesus.

Our growth isn't linear, it's circular. It bends back on itself and overlaps in ridged swirls and curves. We aren't marching forward on a time line so much as we're adding rings to our core like aged oak, firming up roots, breaking bark raw, the shedding of ancient skins, limbs reaching and stretching and yearning for light. We are grafted into a family tree far beyond what we ever imagined when we plotted names on a worksheet and wondered about the empty spaces.

There are droughts and rings like slivers, scratching out our captivity like hash marks on a prisoner's wall. There are monsoons when we soak up the earth and we drink so deeply the atmosphere expands. If we're lucky, we've been paying attention to it all. This is what it means to discover glory. It is not one side of the equator, where the light shines. It is all encompassing, a magnet directing our eyes to see the work of God in our midst.

Children dance in soppy wet puddles and you see a bit of miracle in the aftermath when the storm clouds tuck themselves back into bright blue skies, because you're here to bear witness to it all. The black sky's sorrow and the glory of noonday. And then there are our ordinary days, and those make you doubt growth and glory the most. Because the world expects you to grow forward, march down a time line. Do more, be more, have more. Then you will see the hand of God and his blessings.

If you are #blessed, you've traded in your beater car for a luxury SUV, your one-bedroom apartment and a roommate for a soul mate and a four-bedroom house with walk-in closets situated in a nice neighborhood with good schools. We are a culture of upgrades—always moving forward, moving upward.

But God is not about upward mobility so much as inward expansion. God's kingdom lives in the ever-widening rings, the core and the hollows. God's kingdom growth starts in the dark and hidden places, in holy ground. In a seed busted open and yearning.

I've written about the good days and the bad days. Life with bipolar disorder can make you feel like that's all you'll ever get. The highs and the lows and nothing in between. No steadiness to the rocking, swaying storms. To the dark nights and the blistering days. No respite from the mania and the thoughts that come feverish and frantic. I live my life in cycles a day at a time. We all do, really. Mine are just more noticeable.

Grief can feel like it tore your world open, ripped it end to end so that all you see are the ragged places that once were whole.

Lack can make you feel like there will never be enough. You'll remember the stories of heroes of the faith, how they went out with praise on their lips. How they never faltered. Like Job, saying "Though he slay me, I will hope in him" (Job 13:15). I clung to that verse for years. How would I know the faith of Job? How would I turn my sorrow into joy, my doubt into obedience? How would I hope when it felt as though I were slain by the hand of God? How would I spin gold from the piles of hay at my feet from my house blowing down once again?

Years later I read it again and I saw what I had missed, the next part of that same verse: "yet I will argue my ways to his face." We can be honest that this is not at all what we expected. That death is a catastrophe, a giant cosmic hoax. That we want no part in it. And Jesus would get that look in his eyes, that long, deep remembrance. Maybe he'd even glance at his wrists, at the scars he brought with him even out of the tomb, to remind us all of the cost to his body and soul and spirit, to say, "My child, you are absolutely right."

Josh told me to write the reminders of that. So this is me cut open, rings showing. This busted-open trunk is my altar to remember glory. To remember what it is to put my hope in the Lord. To keep that language of hope fluent on my tongue.

I'm shedding skins and grafted in, abiding in Christ; those rings are expanding, and everything is tender with new growth.

Suffering will visit us all; grief makes its home with the death among us, in us. We revisit our humanity, our frailty, our weakness. We are dust. There are no warranties for the wear and tear we encounter in our lives. Only a promise all will be made new. We hope. We know a God who saves in so many ways. Sometimes he gathers the weak from hospice beds and carries them home. Sometimes he sits with the dying and weeps with them for a little longer, and sometimes he brings them back to life to bear witness to the stories from the edge. To tell everyone there is hope here too. I've seen it with my own eyes. I've lived to tell the tales.

We keep company with sadness. We learn the lament of everyone who holds quietly to the knowing: things are not as they should be. And still we hope. Still we see our Redeemer come. We speak in the dialect of our kin, our native tongue. We are fluent in the language of hope. We bear witness to the goodness of God in the most unlikely places. He is our all in all—we know this from the desperate spaces when we had nothing else. No other route, no calmer sea, no other choice but surrender. And that is a gift. That is our glorious weakness.

Acknowledgments

I am moments away from submitting my manuscript and this is part of the whole shebang. It feels a monumental task to thank the many kind folks who helped me get here, so before I hit Send, let me just say, I could write a separate ebook filled with adulation and praise for the people who selflessly helped these words come. You are my people, my kin and company, my readers and friends. You helped birth this book, so I have you to blame . . . er, thank. Either way, we're in this together.

To Josh, you're the most faithful man I know. Thank you for the calluses on your hands and the ways you've labored in love for me all these years. You always let my cold feet find your warm ones under the covers. Thank you for circling the good garage sales, starting the wood fire for me when the sun hadn't even made it up yet, and for always being home to me. I love you more than I even have words for and goodness knows, that's a lot.

To my mom, thank you for your obedience to the absurd and foolish things in this world. You taught me to believe the kingdom of God would be just so. Thanks for keeping me alive with kimchi fried rice, dahl and curry, and all manner of high-caloric foods and for feeding me books when all else failed. You make the world more beautiful with everything you plant. You're my BFF and not just because you feed me and cut me flowers, although that helps.

To my dad, I wish you were here to embarrass me by telling every random stranger who crossed your path to buy your daughter's fantastic book and that it will change their lives, whether it's true or not. Because in your eyes, it would've been. I miss your stories but our day is coming. I'll see you in the by and by. Save me a seat by the lake and order me some momos. I'll bring James Taylor on vinyl.

To my children, Judah, Kaia, and Nehemiah. You are the joy in my world and I'll never recover from the gift of being your mom. You've all taught me so much. Thank you for being quiet, bringing me endless coffee just the way I like it, and binge-watching shows with me when I couldn't write another word. Thank Jesus you all turned out funny. I don't know what I would've done if you were humor deficient because your laughter is so beautiful it makes my heart hurt. I love that laughter is what we're good at.

To Jordan and Sarah Boston, for hooking me up with a hotel room to write all hours of the night, and for letting me sit and talk it all through in your living room for just as long. I already miss you being down the road and you haven't even left yet.

To Kathi Denfeld, for staying with me during the literal hurricane and some figurative ones too and for being my first writing friend. I'll get the good ice and meet you at Red Robin. Let's wear hats.

To Crystal Clute, for being the best Ms. Frizzle a girl could have. Thank you for the endless ways you serve and love me. I'll even turn the Go Away sign around for you.

To Laurie McAlpine and Kimberly McKaig, you helped me find the lifeline I needed when I was drowning and made sure I had the resources to grab on. You two are a gift.

To Deidra Riggs, you opened the door and said we rise together. I'll always be grateful.

To Tanya Marlow, who gave me a space to tell my story when telling was the scariest thing of all. You helped me be brave.

To Al Hsu, for being a prophet with a spreadsheet. You helped remind me of my somebodies.

To my JumpingTandem road trip friends, Ashley Larkin, Lisha Epperson, Dana Butler, Kathi Denfeld, and Amber Cadenas. That trip began this work and I'd travel anywhere in a minivan with you. Thanks for your honest words and also for not letting me die next to the nacho machine.

To my agent, Don Jacobson, thanks for your gentle pastoral heart telling me to wait until I couldn't not write the book. Those years of rest made all the difference. Your wisdom, expertise, and belief in not only this book but me as an author helped me trust this story is worth telling. I can't imagine this book in the world without your fingerprint on it.

To the team at Baker Publishing who took a chance on this first-time author known primarily for writing her feelings on the internet, it's too late to back out now, so here we go! To Patti Brinks, for creating my beautiful book cover and pouring so much care and attention into every detail, I could not love it more. You had me at gold foil. To my editor, Rebekah Guzman, thanks for seeing something in the very first iterations of this message and for pursuing it. You've been a wonderful advocate for this book and helped me believe it could have a place in this world. To Nicci Jordan Hubert, for answering all my newbie questions, of which there were many, and for helping me not get too carried away with similes. To Julie Davis and Gisele Mix, thanks for putting the commas, dashes, and semicolons where they're supposed to go and for making me look smart.

To my writing sisters—specifically those in *The Inkwells*, *The Chapter*, (in)courage, *The Mudroom*, *GraceTable*, *Redbud Writer's Guild*, Hopewriters '*Let's Talk Shop*', and *SheLovesMagazine*. You told me I could write, you helped me find my voice, and you championed my words like they were your own. I can't imagine writing anywhere but in community with you.

To #teamAlia, who with the mastermind skills of Holly Stallcup, formed on my behalf these last days to champion me to the finish line when I was all out of breath. Thank you for the quotes, memes, GIFs, prayers, playlists, daily emails, gifts, flowers, cuss words, and cards. You were a gift I didn't even know I needed. I will email this to my editor singing "All 4 You" while thinking of all of you.

To Voxer, you are so much better than a phone call or a text message and without you, I don't know how I would've done this work. I'm sorry I ever doubted you. Don't ever leave me.

To my Voxer friends who sustained me during long nights, early morning writing times, and everything in between. Ashley Hales, Cara Meredith, Annie Barnett, Kamille Sellick, Kris Camealy, Adriel Booker, and Shannan Martin, thanks for all the things. You walked with me at different points on this journey and, let's all admit, sometimes dragged me behind you. I'm just glad we're going the same direction. I love you as much as I love the 3X speed option on Voxer.

To Grace Cho, Tasha Burgoyne, and Kathy Khang—it sucks so much less with you. You know what you did. Keep it in the vault. #kimchisisterhoodforever

And lastly, to my faithful readers who've journeyed with me all these years. You met me in my inbox and in messages and comments and reminded me why any of this matters the nine bajillion times I was ready to call it good, buy a pretty journal, and go back to scribbling in it and tucking it under my mattress. You helped me release these words into the world hoping they do a little bit of good. We hold each other's hands and speak this beautiful mysterious language of hope. You help me stay fluent. I couldn't be more grateful.

Notes

Foreword

1. Oswald Chambers, *My Utmost for His Highest*, Classic ed. (Grand Rapids: Discovery House, 2017), November 5.

Introduction

1. This quote is most commonly attributed to Charles Haddon Spurgeon. Goodreads, accessed April 21, 2018, https://www.goodreads.com/quotes/1199735-i-have-learned-to-kiss-the-waves-that-throw-me.

Chapter 1 The Nakedness of Need

1. Augustus Toplady, "Rock of Ages," 1763, public domain.

Chapter 2 The Ransom of Words

1. W. D. Cornell, "Wonderful Peace," Hymnary.org, accessed April 21, 2018, https://hymnary.org/text/far_away_in_the_depths_of_my_spirit_toni.

Chapter 4 I Am Not Labeled, I Am Named

1. Sun Tzu, *The Art of War* (New York: Quarto Publishing Group, 2017), 13.
2. Portions in quotation marks are from Isa. 43:1–3, emphasis added.

Chapter 9 Starving to the Feast

1. All Sons & Daughters, "Great Are You Lord," released April 23, 2013, track 4 on *Live*, Integrity Music.

2. This idea has historically been attributed to St. Benedict. Benedict of Nursia, *The Rule of St. Benedict*, sixth century.

Chapter 10 The God of the Lost

1. Nina Simone, vocalist, "Feeling Good," by Anthony Newley and Leslie Bricusse, recorded in 1964–65, track 7 on *I Put a Spell on You*, Philips Records.

2. Al Hsu, "The Publishing World: Trends, Context, and Where You Fit" (presentation, The Voice Project, Kilns College, Bend, OR, February, 27, 2016).

3. Mary Oliver, "The Summer Day," in *The House of Light* (Boston: Beacon Press, 1990), 60.

Alia Joy is an author who believes the darkness is illuminated when we grasp each other's hand and walk into the night together. She writes poignantly about bipolar disorder, grief, faith, marriage, poverty, race, embodiment, and keeping fluent in the language of hope. She lives in Central Oregon with her husband, her tiny Asian mother, her three kids, a dog, a bunny, and a bunch of chickens. For her blog, visit www .aliajoy.com.

AliaJoy.com

Visit Alia online to learn more about her speaking, subscribe to her newsletter, and much more.

LIKE THIS
BOOK?
Consider sharing it with others!

- Share or mention the book on your social media platforms. Use the hashtag **#GloriousWeakness**.

- Write a book review on your blog or on a retailer site.

- Pick up a copy for friends, family, or strangers— anyone who you think would enjoy and be challenged by its message!

- Share this message on Twitter: **I loved #GloriousWeakness by @AliaJoyH // @ReadBakerBooks**

- Share this message on Facebook: **I loved #GloriousWeakness by @AliaJoyWriter // @ReadBakerBooks**

- Share this message on Instagram: **I loved #GloriousWeakness by @AliaJoy // @ReadBakerBooks**

- Recommend this book for your church, workplace, book club, library, or class.

- Follow Baker Books on social media and tell us what you like.

 AliaJoyWriter

 AliaJoyH

 AliaJoy